A HISTORY OF LUTSEN

GATEWAY TO THE WILDERNESS

R McDowell

By

Robert Mc Dowell

Published by:

Lutsen History Press
(Lutsenpress@lutsenhistory.com)

For Jen and Jill – my heroines

Thanks to:

George Nelson Jr. – for his inspiration and memories

Patti Nelson – for her understanding and clarifications

Willard Nelson – for recording and sharing personal history

Elizabeth Barniskis – for proofreading

Scott Harrison and Nancy Burns – for preserving Lutsen history

Dick Nelson – for his interest, time and help

Darryl Sannes – for sharing military history

Dusty Nelms – Cook County Recorder's Office – for research

Minnesota Historical Society Research Staff – for their availability and knowledge

Mike Larson – for background information and hospitality

George Hovland – for sharing stories

Patsy Ingebrigtsen – Grand Marais Public Library - for research

My wife, Mary – for far too much to list here

Although many people helped create this book, any mistakes are the author's alone.

Table of Contents

CHAPTER 1 - RICH ENOUGH TO GIVE US ALL A FARM

CHAPTER 2 - NORTH SHORE FISHERMEN

CHAPTER 3 - THE ACCIDENTAL RESORT

CHAPTER 4 - WALKING THE PLANK

CHAPTER 5 - LUXURY - BUT NO OUTHOUSE

CHAPTER 6 - BE CAREFUL WHAT YOU WISH FOR

CHAPTER 7 - COLD WATER KEEPS YOU PLENTY AWAKE

CHAPTER 8 - WOW! THERE WAS THE BEAR!

CHAPTER 9 - LAND GRABS

CHAPTER 10 - WE GOT MOOSE, ALL RIGHT

CHAPTER 11 - MURDER STOPS LUTSEN IN ITS TRACKS

CHAPTER 12 - AN ORGY OF WOLVES

CHAPTER 13 - THE OFFICIAL BIRTH OF LUTSEN

CHAPTER 14 - SKUNKED

CHAPTER 15 - THE S.S.COOK

CHAPTER 16 - HOME BREW

CHAPTER 17 - THE ONE-MOOSEPOWER BOAT

CHAPTER 18 - HERRING OR BLUEFIN?

Table of Contents (continued)

CHAPTER 19 - BOBCAT ON MY BACK

CHAPTER 20 - A ROYALE UPBRINGING

CHAPTER 21 - LIGHT BEFORE THE STORM

CHAPTER 22 - FROM FINE DINING TO MESS HALL

CHAPTER 23 - EVERYBODY GOES INTO THE INFANTRY

CHAPTER 24 - BETTER LUCKY THAN SMART

CHAPTER 25 - END OF AN ERA

CHAPTER 26 - FIRE AND DESTRUCTION

CHAPTER 27 - A DREAM COME TRUE

CHAPTER 28 - REDUCED TO ASHES

CHAPTER 29 - BOOM AND BUST

CHAPTER 30 - THE TROUBLE WITH BEARS

CHAPTER 31 - HOT-DOGGING

CHAPTER 32 - A LION, AN ARAB AND SCAVENGERS

CHAPTER 33 - WHAT CAN'T YOU GET AT LOCKPORT?

CHAPTER 34 - THE GEM AT LUTSEN

CHAPTER 35 - MEMORIES

CHAPTER 36 - FAMOUS PEOPLE

Foreword by George Nelson Jr.

I first met Robert Mc Dowell at a conference. I was 85 and my presentation included stories of growing up in the Lutsen area. Robert found the stories fascinating and asked if I had ever considered writing them down for possible publication. I was thrilled because I always feared that Lutsen's history and the stories of the people who settled there would be lost forever when old-timers like me were no longer around to recount them.

The first white man to settle the wilderness area that would become Lutsen was my grandfather, who arrived in the mid-1880s. In those days, most of his neighbors were not people but bears, moose and wolves, although several Chippewa families lived nearby. The Chippewa and my grandfather helped each other, with the Chippewa sharing vital knowledge and skills, while my grandfather provided modern tools, work and education.

Despite the constant struggle to survive wilderness living, my grandfather welcomed many passing travelers into his home. Through his foresight, tenacity and work ethic, this became Minnesota's first and most famous resort.

My father, an outdoorsman and conservationist, covered a large wilderness area as a Minnesota game warden - the last to use a dog sled. He also expanded the resort throughout the very difficult depression years and rebuilt the lodge after several devastating fires.

As a boy, I loved listening to the old settlers tell tales of wilderness life. Often the stories were exciting, sometimes they were funny and occasionally they were tragic. The stories helped me understand what these people had to endure and made me realize how fortunate I was. My experiences in World War II reinforced that gratitude but also gave me the inspiration to build on their legacy.

This book captures the hopes, struggles and achievements of early wilderness pioneers. It also includes the great effort that went into more modern accomplishments such as building a ski resort in the mountains at a time when heavy machinery was not available and much of the work was done by hand or by jerry rigging solutions to serious problems. The environmental challenges of carving a golf course out of the wilderness are also described.

Most people don't realize that, although small in population, Lutsen is an economic powerhouse for the entire North Shore area. This book outlines how that came to be and I want to thank the many people who made it possible by dedicating their lives to Lutsen.

Whether you have never heard of Lutsen or are familiar with the area, you will enjoy reading its history and lore. I promise you will learn something new from the research that went into this book - even I did.

You can still visit almost all of the locations mentioned in the book and see the traces that remain from many of the events described. I hope you will take the opportunity to do that and to explore our beautiful and still-rugged region. I would particularly recommend a trip to the top of Moose Mountain, which can be reached by gondola or by hiking. From there, you will have a spectacular view of countless miles of wilderness that is unchanged from the time of the early settlers. This will give you an appreciation for what they confronted. And who knows? You might even see some of my grandfather's early neighbors...

George Nelson Jr.
Lutsen, Minnesota
March 4, 2012

"Wilderness is the raw material out of which man has hammered the artifact called civilization."

Aldo Leopold

❧ CHAPTER 1 ❧

<u>RICH ENOUGH TO GIVE US ALL A FARM</u>

November 16, 1632 is a foggy morning that finds the Thirty Years War between Europe's Catholics and Protestants raging at full force. Advancing into Southern Germany, the Protestant Swedish Army, led by King Gustavus II Adolphus engages Austrian opposition at Lutzen. With the King leading the charge, the Swedes advance. However, in the early afternoon, the monarch's riderless horse gallops between the battle lines halting Swedish progress and prompting a frantic search for the sovereign. His body is found and secretly removed in an artillery cart, so that his army will not be disheartened by his death. When news of his loss leaks out, however, the Swedish troops are galvanized with calls to *"Avenge the King!"* Sweeping forward, the Swedes force an Austrian retreat. Count Axel Gustafson Lillie, one of the King's generals who survives the conflict, is rewarded for his loyalty with land on which he builds Castle Lofstad, near Norrkoping, Sweden.

The castle estate prospers and over 200 years later, Margarete and Nels Olson are serf-farmers there. On April 27, 1863, Margarete gives birth to the couple's first child. In keeping with tradition, the boy's surname is taken from his father's first name and the baby is christened Charles Axel Nelson.

At age 18, Charles announces that he wants to see America. He has heard about the new land through frantic advertising carried out by shipping companies and land agents. Among their exhortations to emigrate is the chorus:

"We have room for all creation and our banner is unfurled
With a general invitation to the people of the world
Then come along, come along, make no delay
Come from every nation, come from every way
Our lands they are broad enough, don't feel alarm
For Uncle Sam is rich enough to give us all a farm."

Charles is impressed and later quotes this refrain to encourage others to come to the part of America in which he finally settles. He also hears stories about America from neighbors with family members or friends who have emigrated and now write back to the Old Country, extolling the opportunities available in the New World. Charles' imagination and ambition are ignited.

Naturally, Charles' family, now including two envious brothers, worry that they may never see him again but thinking he can do better than be a serf, they support his ambition. Encouraged, Charles steps off Swedish soil and for the first time, boards a ship.

Charles Axel Nelson about age 18

The cheapest regular fare from Gothenburg, Sweden to St. Paul, Minnesota is about $54 (almost $1,200 today), although substantial discounts are offered to immigrants. Charles' journey is like that of millions of other emigrants. Unable to afford a cabin for the Atlantic crossing, he suffers the discomfort and privations of steerage passage, so called because the accommodations are between decks, where the controls to steer the ship are located. (Although some speculate wryly that steerage really refers to the treatment of passengers as cattle, or steers).

For the voyage, Charles must provide his own mattress, blankets and eating utensils. He shares an area of about 60 feet by 12 feet with at least 50 other travelers. His sleeping space is no more than two feet wide with a temperature close to 100 degrees. He has to endure an overpowering stench from toilets, decomposing refuse and reeking fellow passengers who have never seen a bathtub or shower. Even more intimate travelling companions are rats, fleas, cockroaches and lice. The ocean crossing will take as little as six fleeting weeks or may last up to three lingering months, depending on weather.

Unappealing as all this sounds, Charles is fortunate. Many of his fellow passengers succumb to the rigors of the voyage. Instead of arriving in a new land awash with opportunity, these unfortunates end up wrapped in a scrap of dirty sailcloth and bound to a board before being jettisoned into the cold, dark Atlantic Ocean.

Entering New York harbor, Charles is euphoric that he can finally see America. At the same time, he feels tremendous trepidation about the immigration process at the Emigrant Landing Depot at Castle Clinton. (Ellis Island will not open until 1892.) Will he be rejected when he tries to register? What if he fails the required medical inspection? Even if he is allowed into the city, will he be able to find reasonable and safe lodging? What about dependable and affordable transportation to his final destination? These are worries enough but Charles faces an extra challenge – he cannot speak a word of English.

Nonetheless, Charles clears the immigration hurdles and makes his way to Minneapolis. He is following thousands of other Swedes who settle in Minnesota because its cool climate, vast forests and numerous lakes remind them of home. The settlers are responding to famed Swedish novelist Fredrika Bremer, who, after a trip to the state, asks: *"What a glorious new Scandinavia might not Minnesota become?"*

Charles finds work as a carpenter and mason. After a while, he lengthens his name by adding another initial, so that he becomes Charles Axel A. Nelson. The new initial does not represent a name but serves to differentiate him from the many Charles A. Nelsons residing in Minneapolis, some of whom are of more than passing interest to the authorities. It may have differentiated him from many more than that since, years later, Charles' grandson, George Nelson Jr. would maintain that his grandfather received a letter from Sweden, addressed only to "CAA Nelson, Minnesota, U.S.A."

On October 12, 1885, CAA, as he becomes known, marries Anna Matilda Peterson, a young immigrant from the Swedish province of Smaland. After about a year, the couple moves to Duluth and CAA obtains work as a crew member on the Evaston, a small fishing boat owned by the Booth Company. Eventually, he becomes captain and receives a percentage of the revenue he generates. Sometime after that, his employer offers to sell him a small boat and fishing nets on easy credit, if he agrees to sell his catches to the company.

CAA has another opportunity to consider. Alfred Merritt, a mining entrepreneur, tries to get CAA to help develop Merritt's claims. However, aware that all that glitters is not gold, CAA is lured to the Booth fishing offer instead.

(Merritt goes on to mine iron ore successfully on the Mesabi Range and amasses a fortune. Within five years, however, he loses it all when creditors demand repayment of loans and Merritt company stock becomes worthless.)

On April 12, 1886, after meeting the five-year residency requirement, CAA becomes a citizen of the United States.

Robert Mc Dowell

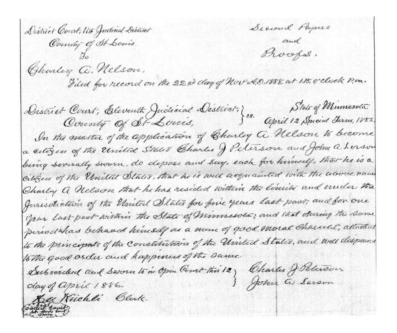

CAA's citizenship application

Witness statements regarding CAA's eligibility for citizenship

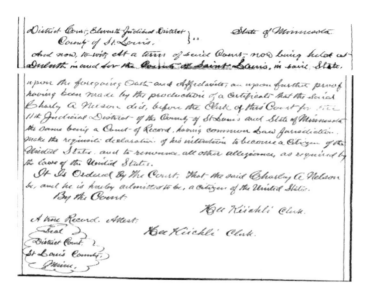

CAA's citizenship court record

As he fishes Lake Superior, CAA explores the shoreline, looking for a spot to homestead. During inclement weather, he is forced to shelter in a small bay at the mouth of a river.

He thinks the bay would be a perfect homestead site. Unfortunately, two other settlers claim to own the land. One is a Frenchman, who disappears soon after making his claim known to CAA. The other is a man named Wheeler, captain of a small tugboat. He is more serious about his claim and drives CAA off the land.

Thinking it odd that two people claim the land, yet neither has built a home, CAA goes to the Duluth land registry office in September 1886, to determine the status of the land. Captain Wheeler has indeed filed papers but has missed the deadline for presenting proof of his claim. Accordingly, the land is available upon payment of $14 (about $275 today). This is a little less than the amount CAA has in his pocket and he promptly purchases the land.

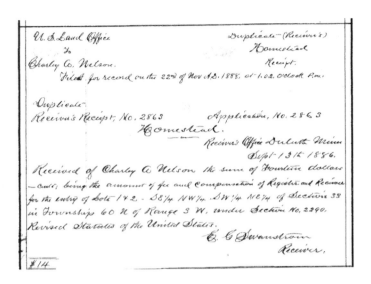

CAA's "homestead receipt"

Elated at his good fortune, CAA quickly builds a small knockdown shanty at his Duluth home on Park Point and hauls it to the Poplar River site on his boat. Although the small bay provides shelter, he has to tie the boat to trees on the riverbank so it will not be swept into Lake Superior by the river current nor be blown upriver by wind off the lake. Clearing trees, he creates space for the shanty, which is assembled by inserting wooden dowels to hold the floor, walls and roof together. The shanty will provide adequate shelter while CAA builds a cabin on a hill above the beach, which at this time is not gravel and pebbles as it is today. Those stones wash down the river after its banks are dynamited to build a railroad years later.

CAA's cabin is similar to the homes of other settlers along the shore. It is built with the logs upright, rather than horizontal, since the latter style is an American design not initially adopted by many settlers. The structure measures about 12 by 14 feet, with a height of around eight feet. It contains a cast-iron stove with a chimney going through the middle of the roof. Furniture, made by CAA, comprises a bed, a storage chest, a cupboard for household utensils, a table and a pair of chairs.

Back in Duluth, in March 1887, Anna gives birth to a boy, Carl. In June, mother and baby join CAA at the river home. A few Chippewa families live in the area and the Redmyers, a Norwegian family, live 13 miles west. There are no neighbors between the Nelsons and Grand Marais, 21 miles east.

The Chippewa spend their winters on a bluff overlooking the bay and their summers on Caribou Lake, a few miles away. They are indirectly responsible for naming the river because they identify it as having "...many aspen trees growing on both sides near its mouth." Aspen is more commonly known as "poplar" in Sweden. Hence, the river becomes known to settlers as the Poplar.

A year later, CAA finishes building a new house and the family moves into that. The cabin becomes the home of CAA's parents and brothers, August (Gust) and Alfred. CAA had sent for the family and they arrive on the North Shore earlier that year. Before long, Gust sets up his own homestead one mile east of the Poplar and Alfred establishes a home one and a half miles beyond that. (The original cabin will later be used by the family as a blacksmith's shop.)

When in his parents' company, CAA speaks only Swedish, not expecting the old folks to learn a new language. With everyone else, however, he speaks only English, believing this essential if he is to prosper in America. He sometimes cannot pronounce English words but can spell them and is usually able to make himself understood. As son Carl grows older, he translates for his father, when needed. (Carl learns a third language when he is about 15. There are no Danish settlers before then and when they do arrive, they cannot speak English and refuse to speak Swedish. So, Carl learns to speak Danish.)

CAA with wife Anna
and
children (left to right) – Ida, Carl, and Hilda

❧ CHAPTER 2 ❧

NORTH SHORE FISHERMEN

CAA initially sticks with his original business of commercial fishing. This requires building a boathouse with a boat slide next to it, a fish house, a dock, large wooden reels for drying, repairing and cleaning nets and, of course, suitable boats. At first, he buys and hauls lumber from Duluth to build the boats. Skiffs, small flat-bottomed open boats with high, pointed bows and sterns, are inexpensive to build and can be used with oars or simple sails. Usually measuring between 18 and 24 feet, a skiff can carry 1,000 pounds of fish and the vessel's design allows it to ride high waves. Later, larger Mackinaw boats, with higher, pointed bows and sterns are built.

Skiff

Targeted fish include lake trout, whitefish and ciscoes. Many sturgeons are also taken but are soon fished out. Initially used as baitfish for lake trout, herring will eventually become the leading commercial fish.

Fishing involves rowing one or two miles offshore to set nets. These attach to buoys that float on the surface, keeping the tops of the nets suspended below the water, like tennis nets. About 100 yards long and hanging seven feet deep, the nets run parallel to shore, with several strung together form a "gang." The bottoms of the nets are usually tied to flour bags filled with rocks that act as anchors, holding the nets in place. When the nets are raised to collect the catch, the anchor bags are cut free. Since this usually happens every other day, anchor bags and rocks are continually replaced. If no bags are available, anchors are made from rocks to which nets can be tied.

Suitably shaped rocks are highly prized and the story is told of one fisherman who finds a treasure-trove of such rocks and deciding to keep a supply at his cabin, fills his boat with the stones. Alas, when he is almost home, a wind springs up and his boat takes on water and sinks. (Presumably, the fisherman survives or we would not know the story.) There is irony in this, because anchor rocks sometimes serve to keep fishing boats afloat. If caught in a storm, a boat can be tied to a net buoy, allowing the rocks to serve as boat anchors, enabling the small craft to ride out wind and waves.

Fishing by boat continues during winter. Usually, two men push a skid, or log platform, with a boat on top, across the ice to open water. Sliding the boat down the skid and into the water, the men jump aboard. If the temperature is significantly below freezing (20 to 30 degrees below zero is often the case), the men warm their hands by dipping them in the water, which is a few degrees above freezing and therefore, comparatively warm. Mounted on the skid is a windlass (winch) holding a cable that hooks into an eye in the boat's bow. When the day's fishing is over, the boat is winched out of the water and back onto the skid. A woman often performs the winching while the men pull and guide the boat.

Boathouse with windlass on Lutsen beach

Winter fishing

If the ice is too high or extends too far from shore to launch a boat from a skid, fish are caught through the ice. A long, thin tree trunk with a line attached, is pushed through a hole cut in the ice. The pole floats beneath the frozen surface but can be seen through the clear ice. A hole is then cut through the ice at the other end of the pole and the attached line is used to pull a gill net into position under the ice. This is repeated, with nets strung together to cover a long distance.

Nets are usually retrieved the day after they are set. To pick captured fish from the nets, fishermen use one hand to grip the fish near its gills while the other hand twists the fish and pulls it free of the net. Because of this strangling motion, fishermen are known as "herring chokers." The nets are laid out again and the fishermen return to shore to prepare their catch for market. Live fish are dressed as fresh. Dead fish are gutted, then packed and salted in 100lb kegs. In winter, fish are laid on the ice to freeze before packing. Fish are shipped to Duluth by steamboat and from there sent to markets in Minneapolis, Chicago and other big cities.

Ankle-deep in herring before packing for shipment

Another method of fishing is with a hook line. This is a horizontal line, from which other lines baited with herring hang down into the water. One drawback with this is that loons, partial to herring, dive down to eat the bait. While a single horizontal line can yield up to 500 pounds of trout, it can also snag a dozen loons and many of the hooked birds die.

Riches are seldom forthcoming for fishermen, especially since economic forces dictate that as more fish arrive at market, prices drop. Despite the backbreaking and life-risking effort involved in their trade, fishermen are often paid less than one cent per pound for herring. To put this in perspective, in 1900 ham costs 11 cents per pound and a pound of lard costs nine cents.

Sometimes, to secure a better price, CAA and his brothers row over 80 miles to Duluth to sell their fish directly at market. This allows them to earn up to five cents per pound of fish. Such a trip takes several days and involves pulling their boat ashore to sleep, eat and rest. CAA tells though, of one trip home with Alfred when they leave Duluth at 8 a.m. and arrive home at 7 a.m. the following morning, after 23 hours of steady, nonstop rowing.

Trips, however, can also be slow and dangerous, especially when bad weather is encountered. CAA recounts one such trip that involves what he considers a miracle. This time, all three brothers make the trip to Duluth, purchase some supplies and make it back to Two Harbors without incident. The remaining 64 miles to get home, however, takes them *"... eleven days and ten nights of struggle with ice and unfavorable weather...,"* according to CAA. For three of those days the brothers are marooned on an ice field and run out of food. CAA notes that, *"If it had not been for Gust, who was lame, we would have walked home but we stuck it out..."*

The miracle occurs when the Lake Superior ice fields crack and an injured trout breaks the surface. The brothers can hear the fish flapping around in the patch of open water and can see the ripples caused by its exertions. Worse, the men imagine the smell of the fish cooking over a wood fire, the feel of a hot meal warming their cold hands and the taste of sweet, juicy meat on their tongues as warm juices run down their chins. Ravenous as they are, though, the brothers face a dangerous gamble.

Old ice can be up to three feet thick and easily support a person's weight. Newly formed ice, however, might be less than four inches thick and not able to support a man. There is no way to tell old ice from new, especially when snow covers the ice. Hence, the trio must risk the ice supporting their weight while they retrieve the manna that is tantalizingly within their reach. They each take a long, thin branch from trees on shore. Held across their chests, the branches will prevent them going all the way through a hole in the ice. The branches are also a safety line between the men, so that if one does fall through the ice, the others can pull him out. In this manner, the men inch their way across the ice to where the fish still flails in circles. They go in reverse order of birth, which has nothing to do with age but everything to do with weight. The youngest, Gust, is lightest and goes first, followed by Alfred then CAA. Holding Alfred's branch with one hand, Gust uses his own branch to guide the fish to the edge of the ice. Despite his lameness, he reaches down with one foot and scoops the fish onto the ice. The whoops of joy from his brothers may have been heard in Duluth. The men devour the trout but afterwards, again go several days without food. Apart from concern about their own situation, the brothers worry about their families waiting for them, who would know by now that something bad has happened.

Finally, however, the ice breaks open enough that the brothers decide they can take their chances and set off for home. Despite their weakened condition, they are able to row across open water. When they encounter an ice field, they pull and push their boat across it to the next stretch of open water. In this hopscotch manner, they finally make it home.

Lake Superior ice field

The dangers inherent in fishing Lake Superior are captured in a verse from "The North Shore Fishermen," written in later years by renowned North Shore visitor Ernest Z. Wanous:

"They go to work on surging waves
Often ride o'er lost men's graves
Men who died in a storm-tossed boat
Battling to keep their craft afloat
On a bed of rock, the crumbling forms
Rest far below the waves and storms
Each tragic end becomes a sign then
Amongst the North Shore fishermen."

🐾 CHAPTER 3 🐾

THE ACCIDENTAL RESORT

CAA augments his fishing income by trapping bears and selling the meat. The preferred method is to shoot a moose, lay brush over it and put a bear trap on either side. Using this technique, CAA can trap 25 to 30 bears each spring and ship the skins to Booth via a steamboat that delivers and picks up supplies along the shore.

Besides fishing and hunting, the Nelsons find they need to accommodate a steady stream of summer visitors. These include foot travelers, boaters, fishermen, hunters, prospectors and homesteaders. Many of the latter are veterans of the Spanish American War, on their way to their own claims in the backwoods. They usually come by boat and need a place to stay until their own accommodations are built. After a few years, CAA builds a small sawmill that enables him to construct houses as well as boats and in 1893, he erects a new house for his family, with additional rooms to house his frequent visitors. Many return as paying guests, making Minnesota's first resort an important and reliable way for the Nelsons to supplement their uncertain income from fishing and hunting.

Of course, these guests need food. Since fresh produce would rot before it could be carted from the nearest market in Grand Marais, the Nelsons depend on their own garden for fresh fruits and vegetables, mainly berries, potatoes and carrots. Located where the swimming pool is today, the garden is of similar size. Meat comes mostly from hunting and fishing, with only pork purchased. One "special" offered to guests is *"All the herring you can eat for one dollar!"*

The original house is to the right. The new house, with upstairs rooms for guests, has a curved porch and a bay window.

Guests occasionally need dental and medical care but there is no dentist or doctor nearby. Hence, those needing a tooth pulled must rely on CAA using forceps to make the extraction. In a small back room of his general store, CAA pulls many bad teeth for family, neighbors and visitors. Whisky is the anesthetic offered to men. Women and children, however, have only caring arms to hold them while an excruciatingly stubborn tooth is twisted and turned before being ripped from its roots. Although he has no medical training, CAA keeps a small medical kit handy and gives first aid for cuts, infections, frostbite, and other ailments. He also puts splints on injured arms, fingers or legs. If there is nothing else he can do, CAA provides a bed until a boat can take the sufferer to Duluth. There is no charge for these dental or medical services.

Supplies unobtainable locally, such as flour, salt and sugar, arrive by an erratic steamboat service, operated by Booth. The company uses a small, coal-burning tug, the "T. H. Camp," to deliver supplies and pick up catches of fish along the Superior shoreline.

❧ CHAPTER 4 🐾

WALKING THE PLANK

The steamboat "Dixon" replaces the "T.H. Camp" in 1888. Faster and with first class passenger accommodations, the Dixon can make two trips along the shore each week, on Wednesdays and Sundays. Since there is no deepwater dock at the Nelson's Poplar site, the Dixon sounds its whistle about a mile from the resort and CAA, usually with one of his brothers, rows out to meet the boat. This is not always easy. CAA once rows out amid waves that carry his boat over a huge rock that could easily smash the small craft to pieces. The waves are so big that CAA does not even see the rock until he is over it. Amazingly, there is not even any water in his boat, except perhaps CAA's cold sweat when he realizes what he just avoided.

Building the dock

Meeting the steamboat
*The winch hauled cargo from the skiff up onto the flatbed trailer that ran
on railroad tracks up to the beach.*

Steamboat Winyah at dock

On reaching the steamboat, the first order of business is to load the fish that have been caught. These must get to market while still fresh and if not loaded on this trip, will spoil. Packed in 100lb boxes, the fish are hoisted from the skiff onto the steamboat. This requires careful coordination between the steamer and the smaller craft, especially in heavy waves. The steamer holds a steady course and speed, in line with the shore. The skiff draws close enough to allow a line to be attached from the skiff's bow to a stanchion on the ship. This holds the skiff under the ship's hoist. There needs to be two men in the skiff, one to stop the skiff from banging against the side of the larger boat while the other hooks boxes of fish to the hoist ropes.

After the fish is loaded and weighed, groceries, clothes, hardware, lumber, furniture, farm supplies, fishing supplies and other merchandise are transferred to the skiff. The quality of beef, pork and ham cannot be guaranteed and the meat is often spoiled on arrival. Among the deliveries are 54-gallon drums of gasoline. These require extra careful handling since, if one drops, it will crash through the skiff.

Also risky is the disembarking of passengers. These travelers must leap from an open hatch in the side of the steamboat into the skiff. If distance or timing is misjudged, the jumper ends up in the cold lake. Livestock such as horses and cows are pushed down a gangplank that extends through the same hatch used by alighting passengers. The plank is then tilted so that the animals are dumped overboard to swim ashore. At the Nelsons' resort, there is no record of an animal being lost this way. Because they cannot swim, chickens are spared dunking.

A good deal of the supplies and merchandise that is dropped off is stored in a warehouse on the beach until it is picked up by its owners. CAA does not charge for pickup from the boat or for storage.

On return trips, the steamboat picks up freight and passengers, along with any more fish. On these occasions, the 300 feet of Lutsen beach are covered with freight.

In rough weather, steamboat loading and unloading sometimes results in the small skiffs capsizing or being swamped, with everything and everyone onboard dunked into the icy Superior water. Luckily, this also is never known to happen at the Poplar River site.

Steamboat service stops in early December because of ice and begins again in mid-April. Of course, this schedule is at the mercy of the volatile Lake Superior weather.

🐾 CHAPTER 5 🐾

<u>LUXURY - BUT NO OUTHOUSE</u>

Locals making their first trip on a steamboat are awed by the luxury offered, compared to the homesteads they live in. Theodore Tofte, an early and prominent settler, encounters this on his first trip aboard the "America" with his father, mother and two siblings:

"I was four years old that summer. When we got on the boat, I remember well my puzzlement over electric lights and the luxury of everything, even carpeting.

We had not been on board very long before I became worried because I had realized the lack of an outhouse in this setup and I knew the time would come when there would be need for such facilities. Somehow, the worry precipitated the need and so I went to my dad to seek his help. I could foresee several impossible solutions but dad took me and my older brother Andy, to show us our first modern toilet facility.

Each of us was placed in a stall with instructions. In short order, I was through and started looking things over. I noticed a chain with a wooden handle hanging from near the ceiling. I finally decided to give it a yank but that was a mistake because all of a sudden, all heck broke loose and water came gushing down as if Lake Superior itself were rushing in.

I figured I had really busted things up and I dashed out of there in a hurry to my dad, in the outer waiting room but I said nothing. Soon, Andy came out too and then dad said he'd show us what more to do. So, he took us to Andy's stall and then he pulled the chain just as I had done and the same thing happened. Andy looked in awe and wonder and then dad said we'd go to my stall. Then I said I already did it.

I'll never forget the look of admiration on my brother's face as he said, "How did you know?""

❧ CHAPTER 6 ❧

BE CAREFUL WHAT YOU WISH FOR

A sign of the growing importance of the Poplar River settlement is the establishment of a post office at the resort in 1890. In his application, CAA states that the post office will serve 25 persons. He proposes to use the name "Poplar" but postal authorities want a less common name, so CAA finally settles on Lutzen, after the 1632 battle.

The building housing the post office is a two-story structure that also serves as a general store. The resort's hired men sleep in the upper level. After a while, the post office moves to where Lutzen's two entrance roads intersect. At this location, the post office is a small building with a bedroom in the back. Gust, a lifelong bachelor, moves in there, eating all his meals at the resort. There is no postmaster salary but incumbents earn commissions on the stamps they sell.

Passenger and Mail sleigh at the Post Office

Mail is delivered on a weekly schedule. John Beargrease, a Chippewa from Beaver Bay, is the most famous of the North Shore carriers who deliver mail faithfully until 1890, when the steamboat "Hiram R. Dixon" is awarded the mail contract.

From December to mid-February, when the Dixon docks for winter, deliveries revert to rowboat. After that, even a rowboat cannot make the trip and dogsleds take over until mid-April. Local inhabitants know mail is about to be delivered when they hear the sound of bells that the sled dogs wear to deter wolves, which are a particular concern to Beargrease, who could be snowbound for days. By Mid-April, steamboats can again ply the waters but sometimes during spring, a Pony Express type of service operates with carriers on horseback bringing the mail in saddlebags. This can be a dangerous undertaking. Mail carriers must cross many rivers and streams. If they are lucky, settlers will have built crude bridges using fallen trees but these often wash away during spring runoffs and heavy rainstorms. When confronted with this, carriers must find a place to swim the horse and mail across.

On April 26, 1908, 22-year-old mail carrier Caleb E. Carlson arrives in Lutzen on his horse and delivers the local mail to postmaster CAA. In exchanging pleasantries, Caleb confides that he has just broken up with his girlfriend and if he were granted just one wish, it would be to *"...never again see the town she lives in."*

Caleb soon learns he can go no further on his route because spring runoff has washed the Poplar River Bridge into Lake Superior. Dedicated to his work, Caleb takes seriously the creed that *"neither snow nor rain"* nor raging rivers will prevent him from delivering the mail with all speed. He therefore refuses to accept that a mere river can delay him and decides to cross the Poplar on horseback. Owner of a stubborn streak, Caleb cannot be dissuaded. Reluctantly, CAA comes up with a plan to have the mailbags carried a half mile upstream where a fallen tree crosses the river. A local man, White Sky Gesick, volunteers to cross the log with the mail and deliver it to Caleb on the east side of the river. This plan will keep the mail safe and dry if Caleb has trouble crossing. In addition to the high, rushing water of the river, mighty Lake Superior is boiling, riled by a strong northeasterly gale. Waves pound the beach, sending tentacles of foam and spray into the air, clawing to drag away anyone foolish enough to venture within reach.

After picking a spot to cross, Caleb finds his trusty steed not quite so trusting. The animal has to be forced, hoof inch by hoof inch, into the rushing river. In mid-stream, the frightened horse rears, spilling his rider from the saddle, one foot caught in a stirrup. Man and animal struggle against the powerful current but the rushing water sweeps them into the frigid, angry lake. As a large wave picks him up, Caleb yells to the men on the beach to save his horse. The young mail carrier is then folded into the wave. The horse battles the churning water and manages to finally gain the safety of the beach. Men rush to grab his bridle and lead the stumbling creature to the Nelson barn, where he is dried and blanketed.

Caleb Carlson is not so fortunate. CAA and son Carl launch a skiff to attempt rescue but find no trace of the young man. Although Lake Superior is renowned for not giving up its dead, Caleb's battered body is found several days later on a beach two miles west of the Poplar. The corpse is covered with gravel, with only toes sticking through. The mail Gesick carried across the river is eventually delivered to Grand Marais.

The death of Caleb E. Carlson is recorded in the Register of Deaths in the Cook County courthouse in Grand Marais. He is buried in his hometown of Two Harbors.

🐾 CHAPTER 7 🐾

COLD WATER KEEPS YOU PLENTY AWAKE

Regular steamboat service contributes to the rapid growth of Cook County and in June 1891, the county's first newspaper, the Cook County Pioneer, is published in Grand Marais. In keeping with his desire to see the county prosper and grow, on June 6, CAA writes a letter to the editor, stating, *"I was very much surprised to receive a weekly newspaper published in this county, and I hope you will succeed. Enclosed please find $3 for one year's subscription to your fine paper..."*

Below the published letter, the editor makes the following observations:

"Mr. Nelson, although a young man, is the old pioneer of Lutzen and Post Master at that place on the north shore 20 miles west of this place. He has a comfortable home, beautifully located, with good barn and outbuildings, and a splendid garden. He is engaged in the fishing industry, which brings in good revenue. There is also a fine sandstone quarry located on his land, which is valuable. He is independent today, while six years ago he just had funds enough to file on this land and build a shanty. This shows what perseverance, frugality and industry will do in Cook County."

How dismaying for CAA to find that his perseverance, frugality and industry may have been wasted. After all the time, effort and resources he has invested in his property, a legal problem arises when Captain Wheeler lodges a claim to the land. After several trips to the Duluth Land Office, the legal issues are resolved and CAA emerges with clear title to the land.

Another sign that Lutzen is gaining stature among North Shore communities is that in 1893 the Pioneer begins publishing a regular column of "Lutzen Items." These are news briefs devoted to the town and its inhabitants. CAA is not shy about stoking this interest in Lutzen by praising the virtues of the area in an attempt to attract more settlers. On November 11, 1893, the Pioneer publishes a long letter from him that states, among other things, *"The past summer, a large number of settlers have arrived here, and located in the surrounding country on timber and mineral lands: and there is room for many more. Truly, Uncle Sam's rich enough to give us all a farm and Lutzen is the place to come."*

His unabashed self-promotion continues, *"The Lutzen House is crowded with guests upon the arrival of every boat, and the weary traveler is well pleased with the spacious rooms, while the meals cannot be excelled... The Lutzen House is now certainly one of the best hotels on the north shore, and a great convenience to settlers."*

The Lutzen House

CAA goes on to list some new business opportunities he is pursuing. One is a large "hennery" from which he expects to ship dozens of eggs to Duluth in the near future. Another involves the planting of a vineyard the following spring. The vineyard will raise *"...the genuine Concord grapes..."* and CAA notes that he is bound to make it a success as he has some very fine ground for the enterprise.

At this time, travel and transportation around the region is either on foot or by boat. Rivers have not been forded with adequate bridges and trails are hardly usable for wagons.

Therefore, CAA also uses the letter to argue for a road he wants built from Lutzen to Gunflint Lake:

"The people of this section think it is high time that a county road should be built from this place to the Gun Flint lake region whereby the many settlers coming here may be enabled to reach their claims in reasonable times with provisions and building material, without breaking their necks or legs. The people of this section of our county certainly have some rights which our county board should respect."

The letter commits the settlers around Lutzen to open a good, passable section of the road through their settlement if the county will undertake to complete the proposed thoroughfare. Such a highway would, of course, add to the number of visitors passing through Lutzen and later, CAA formally petitions the county to build the road. The county commissioners deny his request and instead authorize $60 for a survey crew to begin work on a road from Maple Hill to an area 19 miles west of that settlement.

Not one to give up easily, CAA files an injunction in the Duluth District Court. He argues that Maple Hill settlers have not petitioned for a road, that there has been no public hearing on such a proposal and that there is nothing to justify building such a road. He loses the argument.

On March 29, 1894, CAA and a mail carrier named Koss row a small boat to Grand Marais to visit friends. They leave their boat on the beach. The following morning, a storm blows in, washing the boat off the beach and smashing it to pieces on offshore rocks. As if to rub salt into his wounds from losing the battle to build a road through Lutzen, CAA has to return home by the existing primitive trail.

The following month, the Pioneer reports *"C.A. Nelson, the enterprising proprietor of Lutsen, will fish on the south shore, in the vicinity of Iron River, this season. He has leased the tug, Eliza, of S.B. Swank and will use her to transport his fish to Duluth where he will dispose of it direct to the retail dealers..."*

Notice that the original name "Lutzen" has now been Americanized to the "Lutsen" we know today.

The change of fishing grounds is not successful and CAA returns the Eliza to its owner because, *"...fishing on the south shore was no good and I will be returning to fishing the Lutsen area."*

As the year progresses, other endeavors undertaken by CAA also do not go well. The People's Party nominates him for County Treasurer but he loses the nomination. The same party also nominates him for Superintendent of Schools but he ultimately withdraws his name from consideration.

However, CAA and Anna are acutely aware how important a proper education is for their children. So, in early July 1894, with the assistance of Governor Knute Nelson, who helps obtain an appropriation of $161.48 for the venture, CAA establishes a school. The original class is comprised of CAA's children Carl and Ida, along with six youngsters from two nearby Chippewa families. CAA's living room at the resort (the "Birch Room") serves as the classroom for two years until a proper schoolhouse is built on a nearby hill in 1896. This is a one-room school with a stove in one corner. Pupils stack their lunch boxes around the stove so their food won't freeze.

Getting to school is not easy for pupils, many of whom have to walk considerable distances. One student recalls, *"...there were years when they walked to school. The furthest one that walked was Homer Massie; he had five miles to walk to school, better than five miles, and very seldom missed a day...later they got a covered sleigh and also a covered wagon and they hauled the kids to school."*

The school also catered to immigrants from Norway and Sweden who attended class to learn English. Most of these students were in their 20s and the other local pupils, who were just kids *"...had a lot of fun with them."*

The Birch Room, pictured on a postcard from the 1920s
Note the pedestal table right of center.
CAA created it from a deformed tree trunk.

CAA on the steps of the Lutsen schoolhouse built in 1896

Children's lives, however, involve more than school and play. CAA's son Carl, who is just seven and beginning school, often goes fishing with his father to spots as far away as Ashland, Wisconsin, 50 miles distant. On one such trip, Carl later recalls that on the way home they run into a fierce storm. The boy seeks shelter in the pilothouse with his dad and watches fearfully as water pours down the boat's chimney. Visibility is less than 20 feet and water gushes through the pilothouse windows that have to be open to prevent misting so that CAA can see ahead at all. Already worn out from the day's activities, Carl is terrified by the dark and howling storm lashing around him. With the simplicity of an exhausted child, the one thing Carl says he learns from the experience is that *"Cold water keeps you plenty awake."*

By age 14, all of Carl's time is spent fishing or hunting with his dad or helping with logging, running the store or manning the post office.

Interestingly, Carl would later bring his own son, Willard, on fishing trips. Hard of hearing, Carl tells Willard to *"...listen for the weather."* There are big trees on shore and the wind can be heard blowing through them before it hits the lake. This is called "an off-land wind" and Willard's job is to sit in the bow and listen for any sound of it. There are no cars or trucks buzzing by and if Willard hears a whistle like a wind, he tells his dad. Carl then runs to the stern and hauls up the fishing nets before rowing with all his strength to get back to shore before the winds pick up.

Often, a gang of nets goes straight out from shore for over a mile. If a wind comes up before these nets can be brought in, the fishermen hang onto the nets and pull themselves to shore, net after net. Still, many don't make it and are blown across the lake.

Meanwhile, always willing to undertake new business ventures, in 1895 CAA begins logging cedar near the Cascade River to make railroad ties and telephone poles. Later, he also logs pine. So much wood is removed by these undertakings that CAA eventually accumulates three miles of shoreline simply because he needs the land to provide more timber.

The following year, an important event occurs that will have far-reaching effects on Lutsen and the whole North Shore. Two doctors from Minneapolis come to the area, seeking a cure for hay fever, better known then as "McNamara's Malady." They find relief and recommend that patients visit the area. Later, people also come seeking relief from tuberculosis and the area becomes known as the "fever haven of America." This significantly adds to the number of guests staying at Lutsen. The increase, however, is not entirely welcomed by CAA's wife, Anna.

For as long as the Nelsons have been accommodating guests, Anna has had no help with related chores. She cooks, cleans, does laundry, looks after children, mends clothes, churns butter, molds candles and makes soap, among other things. Also, although the home has running water, this freezes in winter and Anna has to slog through ice and snow that is often five feet deep, to carry water from Lake Superior. If a traveler comes through, snowshoeing or walking or on a dog sled and stops in for a meal, Anna often offers the food for free if the traveler fetches water from the lake. It is not until 1897 that CAA finally hires help for his long-suffering wife.

Some of these travelers are ice skaters, on their way to and from Grand Marais or Tofte or even as far as Duluth. They might skate a mile or more out on the lake and some even use sails to catch the wind.

CAA continues trying to entice new settlers to the area by chartering a boat for an excursion from Duluth to Lutsen. Passengers are prospective homesteaders and the round trip fare is $1, compared to $5 for a trip from Duluth to Grand Marais, only 20 miles further. Meanwhile, a famous North Shore character decides to leave the area when John Beargrease sells his team of four sled dogs for $150 and heads to the Alaskan gold fields.

The Nelsons, however, have already found their treasure. Their prosperity can be gauged from a January 22, 1898 report in the local newspaper (now called the Herald), stating that CAA has been offered $10,000 for his Lutsen holdings but refuses to sell. His political fortunes also look promising when he wins the Republican nomination to be county commissioner for the Second District.

Lutsen's importance continues to rise and on December 3, the Herald recognizes this by publishing the first of a "Lutsen Locals" column dedicated to people and events in the Lutsen area. Unfortunately, the Lutsen correspondent seems less than enthusiastic to share news and on February 4, the newspaper states dryly *"Our Lutsen correspondent would oblige us by thawing his ink bottle."*

This has the desired effect, and another "Lutsen Locals" column appears in the newspaper's March 11 issue. However, the correspondent falls silent again and there are no further "Lutsen Locals" columns for many years.

🐾 CHAPTER 8 🐾

<u>WOW! THERE WAS THE BEAR!</u>

It may seem that the people of Lutsen are living in civilized luxury as the 20th century draws near but they are still in a vast wilderness, dependent on nature's bounty for survival. Settlers with no guns obtain meat with snares. Rabbits are easy to get that way as are other game, including deer and even wolves. Wolves are not eaten but their skins can be traded for groceries or cash. Also, the state pays a bounty on wolves. These payments and the sale of beaver hides are the only sources of income for many settlers. Families learn to can vegetables, wild berries, meat and fish to last through the long winter months. With no refrigeration to keep meat from spoiling, most big animals are killed only in late fall or winter, quickly cooked and packed in jars.

A journey of just 100 miles is arduous. This is highlighted by Gust Nelson's recounting of a trip along the shore from Duluth in 1898, with the first horse ever brought along that route. The road is no more than a wilderness path crossing countless swamps, rivers and streams and is known by many names, including: Shore Road, Old Road, Dog Trail, and Beargrease Trail. Gust sets out on November 1st. The horse is a draft animal, carrying supplies and destined for logging work. It is not suitable for riding, which is unfortunate for Gust since the trip takes four days. At the Manitou River, he is forced to detour miles inland, along the west side of the river and then come back down the east side. The detour alone takes six hours. Finally arriving home, Gust's feet are so badly swollen he cannot wear shoes for four days.

By 1899, settlers along the shore realize they can exercise more control over critical local functions such as tax collection and road building if they form towns. On July 24, the County Board approves petitions granting township status to Grand Marais, Maple Hill and Tofte. CAA is elected chairman of the Board of Commissioners for the town of Tofte, which includes

Lutsen. For this important position, CAA is paid the princely sum of $2 per day (road laborers earn 50 cents more).

By this time, 12-year-old Carl, in keeping with the mature roles children play, has already undertaken his first bear hunting trip with his father.

Trappers have observed for years that bears do not always eat the fish they catch, especially spawning suckers. Instead, bears often leave such fish to rot on land and then return in a few days to eat the maggots that are feasting on the fish carcass. Using this knowledge, trappers use old meat or anything else sufficiently smelly for bear bait. The traps used by CAA are custom-made by a blacksmith friend named Barker, after whom Barker Lake is named. Weighing only eight pounds, the traps are much lighter than commercially produced ones. The traps attach to lower tree branches by chains. Their lighter weight makes the traps spring more easily but has the disadvantage of allowing bears to break off the tree branches and drag the traps away. Carl tells the story of him and his dad following a bear that has broken away:

One time father and I got a bear in a trap and he got out in open country. We had a hard time to track him. He had been in the trap for several days. We came to a place where there was an island of trees and Dad instructed me to go through there and he would go around it to see if he could find the tracks. I get into the swamp a little way, and the first thing I knew, wow, there was the bear. He made a lunge at me. He had the trunk of the drag tree almost chewed off, so when he made for me, it broke off. The bear didn't know that, but I knew enough to holler for Dad. When the bear made his lunge, I turned and skinned the side of my face and I knew enough to stand still. I didn't move and the bear didn't either. He just stood there and turned his head a little. It was maybe two, three minutes before my father got there and shot him.

Checking CAA's traps involves young Carl walking with his dad in a circle of about 50 miles. Within the circle, Carl recalls 35 bears being caught one year and 50 in another. One of these creatures measures nine feet tall, with a 70-inch girth.

On another bear-hunting expedition, CAA, the blacksmith Barker and 13-year-old Carl travel by birch bark canoe to Rice Lake, then head north through the Rice Lake ponds to Crescent Lake, at that time called Pine. With rifles, tents, blankets, axes, cooking supplies and traps to carry, Carl has a heavy pack to portage. The plan is to make base camp on an island at the south end of Crescent. The trap line will fan out from there. The adults are gone three days trap setting and Carl is left alone with a Winchester rifle to keep bears from the food supplies. On his first day alone, a bear swims to the island and Carl shoots and skins it. The following day, he kills a turtle. Having heard that turtles contain seven kinds of meat, Carl decides this specimen will provide fine dining. Alas, the turtle's sacrifice is not appreciated, with Carl later telling people that the turtle meat *"...would have tasted better with some salt."*

When the men return to pick up Carl, they are overburdened with heavy, fresh bearskins. Some of the gear they initially brought will have to be left behind. This equipment is carefully stored under a cedar windfall where it will be sheltered for use on a future hunting or trapping expedition.

Despite the number of bears he kills, CAA may have a soft spot for the creatures, as evidenced by this bemusing item published by the Herald on December 9, 1899:

"C. A. Nelson of Lutsen was in town during the week. Charlie is sitting up nights now trying to get his pet bear to hibernate. He puts it away every night and bids it goodbye, not expecting to see it again until spring but it is up before him every morning."

There is no other indication from public records or family recollections, that CAA ever had a pet bear. Perhaps the wilderness pioneer had a twinkle in his eye and could not resist pulling the leg of the city-slicker editor.

Depending on your point of view and proclivities, 1899 is a year to either celebrate or bemoan a significant action or, more appropriately, inaction, taken by the county board. There are hundreds of loggers in Cook County and the November 25 edition of the Herald reports with alarm that a plot is afoot to open a saloon to cater to their thirst for alcohol. The report states that a stack of liquor has been unloaded from the steamboat Dixon and a tavern is to open at the Hokenson homestead, near Lutsen. The newspaper's editor is vehemently opposed to such an establishment and is no doubt greatly relieved when the County Commissioners refuse to issue the required liquor license.

By the end of the century, the resort is bustling. It is so busy that, to preserve some privacy, Anna is moved from the homestead to give birth to a son, George, on November 20. The birth occurs in a fishing shack on the east bank of the river, on a bluff above the lake. George would later recall that the shack was run by the Crofts in Grand Marais and *"...my mother was taken over there; that's where I was born because there was quite a lot going on, even at that time. We had tourists coming through, like doctors and lawyers and surveyors coming in locating people in the northern part of Cook County, timber cruisers and so forth."*

The rocky point, on which the shack stood, is still accessible from the bottom of the wooden steps leading to the Lutsen townhomes.

❧ CHAPTER 9 ❧

<u>LAND GRABS</u>

Over the years since CAA's arrival on the North Shore, many settlers have drifted into the region, attracted by the generous provisions of the Homestead Act and by advertising literature that describes the area and Cook County in particular, as a place where good crops could be grown. The Act, passed in 1862, allows any citizen or intended citizen who has never borne arms against the U.S. to claim 160 acres of surveyed government land. Claimants are required to improve the lot by building a dwelling and cultivating the land. After five years on the land, the original filer is entitled to the property free and clear, except for a small registration fee. Title can also be acquired after a six-month residence with minor improvements, provided the claimant pays the government $1.25 per acre (about $28 today). This leads to a large influx of Scandinavian settlers around the turn of the century.

A person who claims a homestead can also file a stone and timber claim. Under the Timber & Stone Act of 1878, up to 160 acres of land deemed unfit for farming can be bought for $2.50 per acre. The purchaser is to enter the land exclusively for his own use and no association or entity is to enter more than 160 acres. In practice, large timber companies obtain title to thousands of acres by hiring men to enter 160-acre lots. These are deeded to the company after supposed compliance with the law.

CAA takes full legal advantage of these opportunities by bringing his family from Sweden to settle the land. In this, the family differs from many homesteaders in the area between 1880 and 1890. Advisers employed by lumber companies help these newcomers select "suitable" land and the companies then buy that land for a few hundred dollars more than the settler paid. Many homesteaders pocket their profits from this scheme and head west. This contributes to large swings in Cook County's white population between 1880 and 1890. From just

65 in 1880, the white population increases to 322 in 1885. By 1890, however, the population plunges to just 98. With their seven family members, the Nelsons are directly responsible for over 20% of the county's population increase from 1880 to 1890.

The Twelfth Census of the United States is conducted on June 1, 1900, a date carefully chosen to fall between planting and harvesting times. CAA serves as enumerator for the western half of Cook County, an area that includes *"...Gunflint and the few who lived on the border."*

Since there are few reliable maps, no address lists and no mailing of questionnaires, CAA performs his duties by boating and walking around his assigned district. Indeed, he walks from Lutsen to the Canadian border. With him, he carries an 80-page book of instructions and a "general schedule" of 22 questions. Interviewing residents individually, CAA records their answers on the official questionnaire. He is required to complete his count within 30 days.

For this, CAA receives less than $3 per day. Mileage and other travel expenses are allowed in extreme cases, if the Director of the Census in Washington D.C. previously grants authority. However, it is impossible for the Director to ascertain the topography and density of population in each district beforehand and enumerators like CAA, working in the field, miles from a post office, have no time to obtain the required authority. Nonetheless, aware of the importance of his work and the deadlines involved, CAA incurs travel expenses without authority and is therefore not reimbursed for these costs.

Many enumerators give up their jobs when they realize what is involved. In resigning, one of them says, *"What do you think I am? I have to ask 22 questions for two and a half cents. That's a good job? You can have it!"*

The 1900 Census Form

🐾 CHAPTER 10 🐾

WE GOT MOOSE, ALL RIGHT

Despite his census work and because of the county's refusal to fund a road to Gunflint Lake, CAA builds his own wagon trail from his resort to the headwaters of the Poplar and Temperance Rivers. The trail follows the Poplar inland, curves west of Barker and Rice Lakes, and ends near Brule Lake. There, 18 miles in the woods, CAA establishes a moose-hunting camp. The camp consists of shacks, a barn and sometimes, large tents and comes to be called Camp Nelson. Guests, supplies and equipment are brought in by horse and wagon in summer and by sleigh in winter. The trail becomes known as the Nelson Moose Road.

The Moose Road and Camp Nelson are very important to Lutsen because they allow resort guests easy access to good hunting, which generates significant business for the town. According to Carl, hunters are mostly rich people from the cities and CAA can charge them each $300. In return, he guarantees each guest a moose. However, hunters are allowed only five shots. If they are unsuccessful after that, the hunting guide will shoot the moose. This does not sit well with some local residents who think it unsportsmanlike for a hunter to claim an animal shot by someone else. In later years, as moose numbers decline, this becomes such an issue that these "hunters" are derided in the local newspaper.

One famous hunter who wants to hunt moose at the camp is Teddy Roosevelt. He sends a letter to CAA expressing his interest and asks to meet him in St. Paul. They meet at the Ryan Hotel and Roosevelt states that he wants to hunt on horseback. CAA does not like to ride and tries to discourage Roosevelt from hunting that way. Roosevelt, however, is adamant and finally decides to go hunting out west instead.

The idea of allowing hunters only five shots has nothing to do with a story told about Carl. He grew up with meat on the hoof available year-round. This gets him in trouble at his home early one July morning in 1914.

An early riser, Carl gets up at 5 a.m. to go to his fish house. He wants to pick his nets early because the less time fish are trapped in the nets, the more firm is their flesh. A forest fire has left his land burned and there are now only black stumps and shoulder high brush for acres around. About 300 yards from the house, Carl, scanning the brush, notices something else - a moose! The temptation for fresh meat is too much and he returns to the house for his rifle. It is a long shot and, knowing his gun, Carl aims a little high. A good marksman, he usually requires only one shot to kill his prey. He fires and as expected, the moose goes down. However, Carl is surprised to see the animal arise. He fires once more and the same thing happens! Again, he shoots and again the animal falls, only to get up a third time! Shocked and frustrated at his poor aim, Carl fires until, after the fifth shot, the moose finally stays down.

All this shooting takes place outside the bedroom where his wife has been sleeping. She is now alarmed, angry and frightened. *"What in the world are you shooting at?"* she demands.

Although slightly deaf, Carl has no problem hearing his wife now. Meekly he replies, *"A moose."*

"This is summer! What are we going to do with a moose?"

Knowing he is in trouble, Carl makes his way through the brush to locate his hard-to-kill moose. He returns with a guilty and nervous look.

"Did you miss?" his wife asks hopefully.

Carl whispers, *"No, we got moose, all right."* Reluctantly, he confesses. Five moose had been bedded down and as each one got to its feet, Carl, thinking it was the same moose, kept shooting.

His wife's face turns white. *"You killed five moose! Oh, my God, what are we going to do with five moose?"*

Carl has no answer and it is left to his wife to act. After making a list of people who can be trusted, she goes to the old crank telephone on the wall and begins calling. *"Carl needs your horses and wagon. How soon can you come?"*

Relatives, friends and neighbors are called. Knowing something is up, they quickly respond. There are 5,000 pounds of moose meat to save and with no refrigeration, it can only be kept by cooking and canning. Soon, Carl is sharpening all the knives he has and preparations are made for a major butchering job by the men. The women collect mason jars, cooking pots and spices. Kids haul wood for stoves. Soon, the ranges are hot and moose meat is cooked and then cooled in half-gallon mason jars. All the while, the ladies keep anxious eyes out their windows for the game warden. The closest is in Two Harbors but information travels and children are warned to talk to no one.

That winter, several families have an ample supply of meat to supplement their diet. Over the years, Carl suffers the telling of this story quite few times. Saying nothing, he just grins sheepishly.

Although never yielding five moose at once, Camp Nelson is a highly successful hunting base. Several daily shifts of workers are needed because hunting continues even when some workers leave to haul killed moose back to the resort for cleaning and icing down before the carcass spoils. The haulers debone as much of the moose as possible, taking only pure meat in their backpacks because bones are too heavy. The packs weigh between 150 and 200 pounds and are often carried from up to five miles deep in the woods.

Gathering and storing ice is also a challenge. The resort has an icehouse conveniently located beside its fish house with several inches of sawdust packed into its walls for insulation. It seems logical that the resort would use ice from Lake Superior but this is not the preferred source because cutting ice on the big lake interferes with resort activities and wind often breaks up Superior's ice sheets, making them dangerous to stand on. Therefore, ice is taken from Caribou Lake where it is safer to cut. Ice blocks measure one foot by two feet by the thickness of the ice (at least two feet). Each block weighs about 90 pounds. The blocks are sawn by hand and transported to the resort. It will be years before one of CAA's sons, Oscar, builds a circular saw with a gas engine to help with ice cutting. This makes the task much easier but the blade cannot cut all the way through the ice and the job must still be finished by hand.

In the early 20th century, the U.S. Forest Service adds about seven miles to the Nelson Moose Road so that it eventually reaches Sawbill Lake.

✤ CHAPTER 11 ❀

MURDER STOPS LUTSEN IN ITS TRACKS

The 1900 census determines that Cook County's population has ballooned to 810, inflated by an influx of prospectors looking for gold, silver, nickel and copper and by loggers culling the area's timber resources. The earliest logging takes place near rivers and streams. In winter, horse-drawn sleighs haul the logs to riverbanks. In spring, the logs are floated downriver to sawmills, many of which are powered by water. As timber stands near water become depleted, lumber companies turn to railroads to transport their logs, enabling year-round logging and mill operations, without concern for spring thaws or low water levels.

In 1905, the Lutsen Tie and Post Company, owned by Duluth lumberman John McAlpine, begins building a dock and a lumber mill where the Lockport store stands. Construction of the dock is a considerable engineering feat for that time. After it is built, tugs and barges arrive from Duluth with supplies and equipment to build a hotel and other supporting buildings for what is yet to come. Materials to build a railroad also arrive at the dock. The tracks begin there and continue northwest for several miles to the Poplar River. Oxen and horses are used to lay the rails, which pass where the ski chalet is now located and end at a sawmill on the banks of the dead water of the Poplar. Further upriver, logging camps are established and higher reaches of the river are dynamited to allow logs from the deep forest to be floated downstream. The dynamiting contributes to the formation of the pebble beach at the mouth of the river. A dam built across the lower reaches of the river will catch the floating logs, which will be loaded onto the train, carried to the Lockport dock and shipped to Duluth. All that is needed now is a train.

The first locomotive is brought up by a barge that has a flat deck with rail tracks mounted. The locomotive is placed on the tracks and tied down. Below the deck, the barge can be filled with water to use as ballast. When water is added, the barge sits lower in the water. When water is released, the barge floats higher. When the barge reaches the Lockport dock, the below-deck water level is adjusted until the barge lines up with the dock tracks. The locomotive is then driven off the barge.

The dock at Lockport

The steam engine however, is not powerful enough to make the climb from the dock up the steep hill to the gentler slopes above. So, the engine is returned to Duluth and a more powerful one is brought to Lockport. With the help of pulleys, horses and its own power, this engine makes it up the hill.

Early one morning in 1910, five years after the enterprise begins, train and crew stand by the sawmill, steam up, ready to haul the first load of wood to Lockport. There is great excitement. A dream shared by many is about to come true and Lutsen will be changed forever. The sawmill blades start turning and processing of the first logs begins.

The following day, everything is shut down. Owner McAlpine has been murdered in Duluth. Speculation is that someone does not share McAlpine's faith in the riches to be gleaned from the wilderness and does not want to lose their investment or future income on the Lutsen venture.

The three miles of railroad tracks are hauled to Duluth and sold as scrap. The boilers and other steel equipment eventually go to the World War II war effort. In later years, the railroad trestle burns down. Barn, bunkhouse and cook's shanty stand silent and neglected until time and weather fell them and wilderness creeps over everything. The concrete footings used for the Lockport dock can still be seen in the clear water just west of the store.

The steam locomotive is parked on Nelson property and one day, the Lutsen Town assessor learns of this. A special meeting of the Town Board convenes and levies a "personal property" tax retroactive to the day the engine was parked. When CAA and brother Gust appear before the board to question the tax, they are told that because the locomotive is on their land, they must pay the tax.

Returning home to ponder the situation, CAA reasons that if the locomotive is personal property of the Nelsons, they can sell it. He visits a friend who operates a scrap yard in Duluth. Recognizing a good business deal, the friend agrees to purchase the locomotive and has it cut up and trucked to Duluth. Having survived a trip across the ocean and many storms on Lake Superior, CAA is not about to be sunk by an unreasonable tax.

Meanwhile, lake trout replace dwindling whitefish as the most valuable fish harvested from Lake Superior. Herring are also caught but are worth so little that larger boats like the America prefer not to carry them because they are not worth the space they take up. This creates a niche for smaller, tug-like boats, 40 to 50 feet long, whose main mission is to pick up fresh and salted herring in the summer and frozen herring in the winter, for delivery to wholesale companies in Duluth. There are between 15 and 20 such vessels plying the North Shore, each boat capable of carrying up to 20 tons of cargo. The boats run on gasoline but can also use cheaper kerosene. They have sails for emergencies and for use in winter, to prevent propeller damage from floating ice. This flotilla of small vessels is nicknamed the Mosquito Fleet because the small boats can dart in and out of small harbors and suck off some of the trade from larger boats. They do this by paying slightly more for fresh fish the local fishermen are selling and by delivering supplies such as gasoline and vegetables for slightly less than the bigger boats charge. However, the fleet is replaced by trucks when a road is constructed from Duluth to Grand Marais during the 1920s.

In the spring of 1902, the Booth Company replaces the Dixon with the much bigger America. The America is large enough to contain a gambling hall but also fast enough to make the trip along the North Shore three times a week. Beginning in October, she delivers mail on that schedule, instead of only semi-weekly.

Within three months, the replaced Dixon runs aground on rocks off Michipicoten, Ontario, punching a large hole in her side. On reporting that the old ship has *"...come to grief,"* the Herald notes that the boat *"...ran for many years and seems to older settlers like an old friend."* The old boat is towed to Michipicoten Island for repairs but meets its end just over a year later, catching fire and sinking in the island's harbor.

In late June of 1902, CAA is nominated as the Republican candidate for County Treasurer. He faces two Independent opponents and knows that this will be a difficult battle, requiring much hand shaking. He visits voters in Grand Marais and Maple Hill and takes the America to meet constituents in the eastern part of the county. His canvassing, however, is in vain and he loses badly, finishing last of the three candidates and being bested by a two to one margin. It has been an acrimonious campaign and when it is over, the Herald lectures the candidates *"Now that the election is over, hatchets should be buried."*

The sour taste in CAA's mouth after the election is wiped away when Anna gives birth to yet another son, Oscar, on December 15.

☙ CHAPTER 12 ☙

AN ORGY OF WOLVES

By age 15, Carl is guiding moose hunters on his own, even though his first moose-hunting trip without an adult does not go well. It occurs in the fall of 1902 when CAA tells Carl the family is out of meat. He asks the boy if he and a friend can go to the upper Poplar River to find a moose and offers to let Carl take his father's prized 30-30 Winchester, if he is very careful with it. Carl races off to find his younger Chippewa friend, White Sky Gesick, at the family teepee over the hill. The two friends are boys who think they are men and are eager to prove it. Soon, they have a lunch put together and are hoisting backpacks onto their eager young shoulders.

Following the Moose Road north, they cut through where the Superior National Golf Course is now located, to the dead water of the Poplar. Continuing past Christine Lake, they head for the Rice Lake ponds. Moose are plentiful in this area and the boys find several feeding in the ponds. However, they know better than to shoot a moose while it is in the water, as they have no way to drag it onto dry land. They will need to find a moose on higher ground.

White Sky cups his hand to his ear every few steps, holding up his hand for Carl to halt. Born hard-of-hearing, Carl compensates with keen eyesight and thus the boys make a good hunting partnership. On a slight rise, overlooking young aspen below, White Sky's hand goes up and Carl freezes. The younger boy points to some brush moving and soon a bull moose moves into the open and begins nibbling on aspen buds. The boys creep forward, Carl gripping the Winchester. It is a downhill shot and in his eagerness, Carl forgets that a rifle bullet rises when fired on a downward trajectory. Carefully raising the rifle, he squints through the sights and aims for the heart. White Sky crouches motionless beside him. Carl presses the trigger gently, so as not to flinch when the gun goes off.

The moose is hit high in the shoulder and does not go down but instead quickly melts into the shadows of the deep woods. Over-anxious, the boys rush after their quarry. Blood on the newly fallen maple leaves confirms the hit but the wound does not slow the moose and they follow its trail all afternoon. Experienced hunters would give the animal time to lie down and stiffen up for a final kill shot but the boys are inexperienced and in a hurry.

In the fall it gets dark early in the north woods and frost descends along with night. When they can see only a little way ahead and feel chilled air in their nostrils, the boys realize they will have to spend the night in the woods. Finding a small clearing on the trail, they build a fire and take turns feeding the flames. Eventually though, over-excited and exhausted, they both fall asleep.

White Sky's sharp hearing wakes him in the middle of the black night. The fire has died down to embers and ashes. Hearing brush and branches cracking, the boy's heart races. Yelps and howls follow the crashing sounds and come closer. He is afraid. *"Carl,"* he yells, *"Moose! Wolves!"* His friend awakens just as a huge black form bounds over them, sending sparks, embers and ashes in every direction. Terrified, the boys huddle together with Carl feeling for the rifle.

Howling timber wolves surround them. They are after the wounded moose. Dragging it down a hundred yards away, the wolves begin fighting over whose turn it is to feed. The howling freezes the boys' blood and they pray for the orgy to end.

Finally, daylight creeps between the trees and the wolves melt away to sleep off their gluttony. The forest grows silent. The boys, now considerably older, rebuild their fire and slowly work up their courage. Rifle cocked, they head to where all the noise came from. They find only parts of the front shoulders, head and rack of their hoped-for first moose. Dejected and worn out, the young hunters head for home.

White Sky's father, Jim, and CAA have been worried about the boys and are happy to see them again. Listening carefully, they nod their heads in understanding.

The rifle young Carl carried that day is gifted to him on his 16th birthday. Years later, Carl estimates he killed over 300 moose with it by the time he was 30, with most of the meat feeding guests at the Lutsen resort

❧ CHAPTER 13 ❧

THE OFFICIAL BIRTH OF LUTSEN

In early 1903, fires rage across Cook County. Political passions are also aflame.

The local elections of 1904 carry forward some acrimony from the 1902 contest and things come to a head in Tofte Township. The annual town meeting splits between Lutsen and Tofte on one side, with Cross River and Schroeder on the other. The latter side demands that lumberjacks from the north woods be allowed to vote at the meeting, since the Schroeder Lumber Company employs them and has its headquarters in Schroeder. A few revolvers are displayed at the meeting but calmer heads prevail and the Cross River/Schroeder coalition loses its argument. The Lutsen/Tofte coalition wins five of the seven town seats with CAA's brother Gust elected Treasurer.

The local political hostilities continue and late in the year, the people of Lutsen file a petition with the Cook County commissioners requesting organization of the town of Lutsen along with a new school district. The commissioners grant the request at their April 8, 1905 meeting. On June 19, the town of Lutsen is formed.

One year later, the end of an era arrives for Lutsen when the Booth Company announces that the America will only stop at Two Harbors, Beaver Bay, Tofte, Grand Marais, Hovland and Grand Portage. As the Herald puts it: *"No more would the ship be at the beck and call of every lone settler along the way."*

Meanwhile, an interloper is about to make its presence felt along the North Shore. People welcome the newcomer as a fresh food source but it will have a devastating impact on one of the area's most ancient and prized inhabitants.

Moose has been a source of food since man encountered the animal but the demand for meat from logging camps in the late 1800s and early 1900s cuts moose numbers rapidly. The logging of forests also greatly reduces suitable moose habitat. The interloper, deer, adds to this pressure. CAA does not find deer at the Poplar River site when he settles there but they appear a

few years later. From various reports, deer likely arrive in Cook
County around 1906, after migrating around Lake Superior
from Wisconsin and following logging cuts up the shore. The
Herald of October 20, 1906 notes that people are seeing deer in
the woods, so it must have been unusual. The deer are not a
threat to moose because of competition for food or habitat.
Instead, they carry a disease-bearing tick that is fatal to moose
and decimates their numbers.

Political battles continue for CAA when he runs for Cook
County Commissioner and finishes in a dead heat with Erick
Leonard. The situation is unprecedented and the Herald reports
that the contest will be settled by special election on a date
determined by proclamation of the governor. The county
auditor is not so sure and asks the State Attorney General for an
opinion. The response is that, in this situation, the auditor can
draw lots to determine the winner.

Calling the tied candidates together, the auditor asks if they
are willing to settle the matter by coin toss. Both decline.
Therefore, the auditor puts two slips of paper into separate
envelopes. One slip is marked "Commissioner" and the other is
blank. Lots are drawn to determine who gets to select first. CAA
wins the draw and selects an envelope. The slip inside says
"Commissioner" and CAA is appointed to a four-year term
representing the Fourth district.

Scandal erupts upon one of his first acts as commissioner. At
its first meeting in January 1907, the new board not only
appoints CAA's brother, Gust, to the position of janitor but also
doubles the position's salary to $50 per month. This leads to a
public meeting on February 11, at the Hovland schoolhouse,
where a petition is created, stating in part:

*"We believe that when a member of the county board by his
own vote helps to elect a member of his own family at double
the wage deemed sufficient for the prior year, such member
thereby becomes the agent of his family and ceases to represent
his constituency, the two positions being incompatible."*

The Herald piles on with a February 16 editorial. After
acknowledging that members of the county board are broad-
minded, successful businessmen, it asks, *"Would members of*

the board, in their own private business pay fifty dollars per month for the work a janitor is required to do?"

Apparently, they would, because there is no record of an adjustment to the new wage.

Less controversially, the young town of Lutsen gains stature during 1907.

First, the Lutsen Evangelical Lutheran Church is formed. Initially, services are conducted by the Lutheran pastor from Grand Marais, in a room above the resort's store. However, a women's group, "The Willing Workers of the Central Sewing Society," raises money to build a small church away from the resort, on property owned by Isak Hansen. The building materials cost $128.02 (about $2,800 today). Originally called the "Lutsen Sewing Society," the group previously met at the Lutsen Resort but move to what members deem a more "central" location. Like hundreds of similar Societies throughout the state, the women raise money for community projects by making and selling needlework items, baskets, pies, and such.

Second, a group takes over responsibility for the Lutsen Cemetery. CAA donated land for a burial ground a few years earlier but leftover money from the church building project enables formation of the Lutsen Cemetery Association, which assumes responsibility for the operation and maintenance of the graveyard.

❧ CHAPTER 14 ❧

<u>SKUNKED</u>

By age 11, CAA's son George has already developed a liking for the outdoors. He enjoys heading upriver with a cut pole and some scavenged string, in search of brook trout and often catches fish weighing seven or eight pounds. He also quits school for 30 days during hunting season and by age 14 is a hunting guide.

George does not consider this work, since he loves the woods and often jogs through them. One day, an urgent message arrives at the resort for a hunter who is at one of the inland moose-hunting camps. George heads off to the first camp but learns that the hunter is at another camp. The camps are 20 miles apart by trail but only a strenuous 11 miles apart as the crow flies. Given the urgency of the message, George delivers it by taking the shorter, more difficult route, using as landmarks the drainages, beaver dams, lakes and rocks he recognizes from his time in the forest. In all, he covers about 30 miles to deliver the message. The hunter, a doctor, gives him a $3 tip (about $40 today).

For other recreation, George often hunts alone for partridge and rabbit. He remembers Carl's experience eating turtle and always carries salt and pepper to make a proper meal during these excursions. When pheasant hunting with a group, George always wants to be second in line because the first hunter will startle the bird and allow the second hunter a good shot.

Not that George is a bad shot. He is an excellent marksman, known for one particular feat wherein his younger brother Oscar holds a dime between thumb and forefinger. George shoots the coin from about 30 feet away without injury to his brother. Either this is an illusion the boys practice or Oscar gets some brains and decides not to risk his digits or the boys' parents find out about the stunt and stop it. In any event, the trick is not repeated.

George and Oscar enjoy another activity during duck migration season. When ice forms on Lake Superior, ducks look for open water on their way south. George and Oscar shovel snow off the ice, which is so clear it looks like water to the high-flying ducks. The birds try to land but skid all over the ice, providing great amusement to the brothers.

The boys have other odd experiences involving animals. One day, at age 13, George decides to deal with a skunk that has been wandering through the resort grounds each day for about a week. The skunk sprays a retaining wall, leaving a malodorous stench for resort guests to savor. George has heard that if held upside down by the tail, a skunk is unable to squirt. So, he hides behind the wall, determined to lean over and grab the skunk by the tail before it has a chance to squirt. Surprisingly, the plan works and George manages to grab the skunk's tail and hoist the creature aloft, at arm's length. No spray comes and George is elated - for a moment. He quickly realizes that he now holds an angry skunk that will spray him mightily the instant he lets go of its tail.

Deciding that the best solution would be to drown the skunk, George calls for Oscar to help. While George holds the skunk, Oscar loops one end of a string around the creature's neck. The other end he ties around a rock. With George holding the skunk and Oscar carrying the rock, the brothers head to the long resort dock. At the end of the dock, George counts to three and heaves the skunk as far out into the lake as he can. At the same instant, Oscar heaves the rock. Ducking, the brothers cover their heads. The skunk does indeed squirt in mid-air, creating an oil slick in the water but no one on the dock is hit and the skunk does not bother resort guests again.

To offset the removal of animals such as the skunk, George is responsible for introducing some species to the northland. In particular, largemouth bass are not found in Cook County until George, sometime in the early 1920s, carries a 10-gallon can of largemouth fry into Lake Agnes. After releasing the fish, George leaves a boat and oars for anyone to use. Almost 20 years later, when George's son, George Jr., is 15 years old, he and a friend drive to the lake. From shore, they see 10 to 20 large bass eyeing them. George Jr. tells his dad, who insists they are the largemouth he stocked.

Among the beneficiaries of the stocking is Lutsen guest Walt Williams, an annual visitor and avid fly fisherman. Hearing about the largemouth, he wants to fly fish for them, using the same technique but larger equipment, since he will need to skim the fly across and between fallen logs. Walt is taken to the lake in a used 1937 Buick LTD that has been converted to a pickup by Oscar. Such a vehicle is needed to access remote Lake Agnes. Walt catches some fish between two and four pounds and is happy with the action as the largemouths leap out of the water to hit a fly. However, after eating them, Walt complains that the fish taste muddy.

The Lake Agnes bass are wiped out when the federal government, which owns most of the land surrounding the lake, over-sprays the area for mosquitoes.

Despite his youthful hijinks, George Sr. is not an animal abuser. He is actually a conservationist and in later years becomes a state game warden and is the last one to use dog sleds as transportation.

Although the job often involves camping out for several days, wardens are more tolerant than today. George Sr. admits that he and the other wardens in Cook County *"...knew that people were killing deer to eat but we did not expressly go after those people because they had to have something to eat and there was no butcher shop short of Two Harbors or Duluth. So we didn't bother them. We were mostly after people that were catching brook trout too small and so forth. And for beaver trapping and so forth."*

This tolerance stems from the area's history of settlers facing no restrictions and killing moose and deer for the food they need to survive. This has been a way of life for many years and laws passed hundreds of miles away are not going to stop it until people have other survival options.

Two events of note occur in the Lutsen area during 1913:

First, the Chippewa tell CAA about a lush blueberry field up in the hills. CAA tells George to get some horses ready, each fitted with two fish kegs to be filled with berries. CAA also sends word to Tofte, asking if anyone wants to go blueberry picking. A teenager named Inga Toftey is interested. She later recalls, *"Five of us from Tofte decided to go. We went to Lutsen by boat, the America or one of the earlier boats. At Lutsen, we met George and his dad, then went 17 miles inland to the berry patches. We filled fish kegs with berries. And that's how we met. We were both 13."* Inga is the daughter of an influential settler and her later courtship with George holds potential for creation of a powerful family. (Inga's family had changed their name from the "too-common" Tofte.)

Second, Hosey Posey and Stella Lyght, with several small children, arrive on December 3, 1913, to homestead in Lutsen. They have determination, one dollar and a sack of flour to tide them over. The young black family, originally from Alabama, has read about the Homestead Act and somehow acquires a Duluth newspaper giving information about property in Lutsen. With the help of Alfred Nelson, they survive their first winter. Afterwards, they farm and sell bait and other supplies to fishermen.

Farming, of course, has its own risks, sometimes unexpected. One story is that Hosey was once chased around his barn by his one bull. Being tall, Hosey is able to jump, wrap his arms around the barn rafters and begin screaming for help as the bull's horns lunge at his swinging legs. Hosey's oldest son, Bert, hears the screams and grabs a rifle. He fires at the bull, hitting a hipbone. The bullet ricochets upwards. Now really mad, the bull turns toward the boy, who fires again and kills the animal. Hosey drops to the ground moaning and clutching his rear end. The ricocheted bullet has hit him in the buttocks. Fortunately, it is only a flesh wound and he survives.

The Lyghts prosper and eventually establish the Northern Lights resort on Caribou Lake.

One of the Lyght boys, John, grows up to work for a while selling tickets and acting as a bouncer at the Lutsen ski area. That experience leads to him becoming the first elected black sheriff in Minnesota history.

❦ CHAPTER 15 ❦

THE S.S. COOK

Both good and bad fortune come to Lutsen in 1916. In April, it is announced that daily mail service will begin between Cramer, to the southwest of Lutsen and Hovland, to the northeast. A few days after this good news, however, Alfred Nelson's home is destroyed by fire due to a faulty chimney. Alfred, along with his wife and daughter survive but are able to salvage only one trunk from their possessions. The family has no insurance.

April also sees the U.S. enter the global conflagration of World War I. One side effect of the war is that people take vacations closer to home. Coupled with the ongoing construction of a Duluth to Grand Marais highway, this results in the Lutsen resort having a busy summer. The pressure of handling so many guests leads CAA to conclude that he needs electrical power to make the resort less labor intensive and more efficient. Thus is conceived a hydroelectric plant that will provide electricity to the resort and town, although the plant will not be built for several years.

In 1917, famine in Ireland creates a big demand for potatoes. Some Lutsen residents see an opportunity. They obtain oxen, plow their land and plant the vegetable. Potato bugs are prevalent and have to be picked off by hand since there are no chemicals to control the pest. It is a real fight to save the crop but enough potatoes are harvested to earn welcome additional income. Carl Nelson makes enough to buy his first automobile, at a cost of $480.

The 1917 Ford model T is delivered to Lutsen by boat, with the wheels removed so it doesn't roll around the deck. On arrival at Lutsen, the vehicle is slung over the side of the boat and placed crossways on two fishing skiffs. These are rowed to shore where a gang of strong men pick up the car and carry it to a log barn where it is placed on wood blocks. Other automobiles are also stored here during the winter months. In the spring,

Emil Hall puts the wheels on Carl's vehicle, teaches him how to crank it to get it running and then shows him how to drive it.

The market for potatoes, however, does not last as long as the Ford. Freight costs make the product too expensive to realize a profit.

A Standard Oil gas station opens at the resort in 1918. Located beside the Poplar River, the station serves automobiles and boats. In later years, the building serves as a boathouse that can still be seen today, adjacent to the covered bridge nearest to Lake Superior.

Two of CAA's children join the armed forces when the U.S. enters the war. Son Edwin joins the navy and is assigned to the USS Nereus. Daughter Ida takes the Civil Service exam and goes to work for the Ordnance Department in Washington D.C. After the war, Ida returns to Lutsen and is named sponsor of a ship that Cook County has won the right to name by finishing among the top 14 counties selling Liberty Bonds in the Ninth Reserve District, which encompasses 286 counties.

The local newspaper (now named the Cook County News Herald) of April 16, 1919 reports that:

"Because another ship already had the name, it was impossible for Cook County to give its name to the ship Miss Nelson will christen. As a result, it was decided to name it after the town where Miss Nelson resides."

This belief that the ship will be named Lutsen is reinforced by an April 23 Herald article about how Lutsen got its name. At its conclusion, the article states:

"This is how Lutsen got its name which now in turn is going to be the name for a U.S. battleship if rumor has it right."

Alas for Lutsen, rumor has it wrong. On November 12, the Herald publishes a photograph of the newly christened S.S. Cook, along with a picture of Ida and a copy of a letter to her parents about the launching of the vessel:

GRAND MARAIS, COOK COUNTY, MINN., NOVEMBER 12, 1919.

GOVERNMENT STEAMER NAMED AFTER COOK COUNTY

The S. S. Cook, as it Left the Ways on October 3rd. Insert, Miss Ida O. Nelson, Sponsor.

AS will be remembered this county won the honor of having a Government ship named after her by the record made in the fourth Liberty Loan drive. The ship has now been launched and Miss Ida O. Nelson of Lutsen, who was named sponsor, has duly christened her.

The event of the launching can best be told by the copying of a letter written by Miss Nelson to her parents, Mr. and Mrs. C. A. A. Nelson. The letter follows:

New York City, Oct. 3, 1919.

Dear Dad and Mother:

The good ship "Cook" was launched today and I wish you could all have been here to see it, but as that was not possible I shall give you a little account of the launching. In the first place we had to get up at 5:30 to have time to get breakfast before starting. An hour's ride on the subway and Hudson Tubes brought us to Newark, where a large limousine met us and took us to the Submarine Boat Corporation shipyards.

As I had never attended a launching, it was a big surprise to be handed an immense boquet of American Beauty Roses with long streamers bearing the name "S. S. Cook". Soon the signal was given that all was ready, and I had barely time to break the "precious bottle" across her prow before she was slipping out into the water, soon to swing broadside so we could have a good look at her.

The Submarine Boat Corporation presented me with a beautiful watch bearing my name and name of the boat and date of launching. Wasn't that nice? They also took several pictures of us and the boat, which I will receive later, together with the remains of the bottle. I know the contents were real, because I was generously sprinkled, and got just the weeniest little taste. Wasn't that exciting in the "Great American Desert", where everybody is thirsty?

The "Cook is a merchant boat of 5,350 dead-weight tons carrying capacity and in two or three weeks will be entirely equipped and ready to start on her maiden voyage.

I believe I have told you all the details, but I'll just whisper that it costs a million dollars to build a boat like the "Cook" and she will have to make several trips across the ocean to pay for herself.

Three cheers for the "Cook"!

🐾 CHAPTER 16 🐾

HOME BREW

The 18th Amendment to the United States Constitution is passed on January 16, 1920. From that day forth, the distribution and sale of alcohol is illegal. Drinking alcohol, however, is allowed. Prohibition causes many fishermen on the North Shore to suddenly become very thirsty. The law allows the sale of malt to make home brew and Sears Roebuck offers such malt through its catalog and stores. So, it isn't long until people learn to make their own home brew and everyone has their own recipe. One ingredient essential to successful recipes, however, is a stone crock.

There are always some brewers, of course, who try to get by on the cheap and use fish kegs instead of crocks. Many of these brewers do not want their wives knowing what they are up to and manufacture the brew in their fish houses, where women seldom venture. These brewers save a dollar and manage to enhance their brew with the tastes of wood, fish and salt. Rather than admit their error, they hold their noses and gulp it down anyway.

Other home brewers decide to save dollars in other ways. Wanting power in their beer, they share secret ways to add alcohol to the brew, often guessing when it is time to bottle their beverage. Carl Nelson is such a brewer. He pays for much malt, many bottles, and a capper. Finally, lips salivating, he guesses it is time to fill and cap the army of bottles standing at attention across his basement floor. Unfortunately, the brew is still fermenting and in the middle of the night, the bottles begin exploding. Carl's wife, terrified of the loud bangs coming from below is not placated when she sees shattered glass and beer foam all over the basement and is overwhelmed by a nauseating smell of alcohol.

Carl hides a few of the two-quart bottles that have not busted but when he opens one, yeasty foam comes pouring out. He tries to catch it in a bucket but that overflows, creating another mess. That is the end of Carl guessing about when to bottle his home brew. He spends the money to purchase a gauge that indicates when the brew is ready for bottling.

Bootleggers coming up the shore from the cities bring gallons of moonshine to the area but it is hard to find any for sale in Lutsen. Good Harbor Hill is the place to go. There, the strongest home brew sells for 25 cents a bottle and there is no restriction on who can buy. Adult or child, if you have the 25 cents, you get a quart.

In May of 1920, George cements relationships between two of the most successful pioneer families in the region when he marries Inga Toftey. Inga later mischievously says she just could not wait to be a June bride. The newlyweds spend the summer at the resort before moving to Duluth, where George operates a grocery and confectionery store.

That same year, the wagon trail from Duluth to Grand Marais is finally finished and horses take over delivery of mail along the shore.

The year ends with the first indication that perhaps the older Nelsons are beginning to feel their age. CAA's wife, Anna, goes to Florida for the winter. In future years, CAA will join her in the "sunshine state" during that season. Before leaving, they always host an elaborate family dinner, attended and relished by their numerous progeny.

While at the resort, though, CAA continues work on his hydroelectric plant and in March 1921, he is *"Arranging to put in a dam on the Poplar River and will put in a turbine and dynamo and make a model summer resort and little village out of Lutsen."* Building the plant is quite an undertaking, with workers mixing concrete by hand, using gravel hauled from the beach by horse.

While the power plant takes shape, a greater power occupies Anna. In September, her death is reported in the Duluth newspapers. The reports prove to be dead wrong. An elderly woman does die at the resort but she was a visitor from Minneapolis.

The year, however, does close with a notable death. In December, CAA shoots a moose with the biggest and most perfect horns he has ever seen. According to Tom Storey, a taxidermist from Duluth, it is *"...the largest and nicest head ever brought in Minnesota. It has a sixty-one inch spread and there are forty-two points."*

The moose is listed as having a 62 1/2 inch spread and 44 points when it is displayed as the "Champion of Champions" at the 1932 Chicago World's Fair.

The "Champion of Champions"

CAA feels extremely fortunate to have bagged such a specimen, especially since moose have declined greatly in numbers during the previous decade. Some people maintain that the moose have disappeared because so many beavers flooded so much land that the moose have little to eat and have gone to Canada. Whatever the reason, the moose population declines so much that moose hunting is closed in 1922.

The ban has a severe economic impact on Lutsen. In just one year, thousands of dollars can be earned from guiding moose hunters. In addition, moose are a staple on the resort's menu. Although deer are now much more prevalent and more easily taken, one moose supplies food for up to two weeks whereas a deer lasts only two days. Also, resort diners prefer the taste of moose.

❧ CHAPTER 17 ❧

THE ONE-MOOSEPOWER BOAT

For one particular moose, it is fortunate that hunting closes in 1922. That is when Carl, famous for shooting five moose one day, encounters a moose in need of assistance.

It is a summer morning and with no wind, Lake Superior's surface is flat. Making his way down the hill from his home to his fish house, Carl's eyes rove over the water to where his nets' buoys should be bobbing. Starting about a half mile from shore, the gang of nets extends out about one and a half miles. Carl carefully scans where the net markers should be because if currents are strong, the markers will be pulled underwater, making the nets hard to locate.

This morning, Carl stops and squints at the lake. A puzzled look comes over his face. Squinting harder, he realizes that something is swimming near his nets. It goes in circles and Carl realizes it is either a bear, a deer or a moose.

Returning to the house, Carl wakes his brother-in-law, Art Gravelle, who is visiting for the weekend. They study the moving object for a while before Carl decides to take his skiff and go see what is circling in the water. The outboard motor he uses can neither tilt nor swivel to steer. Instead, the skiff has an old-fashioned manual rudder.

The mystery swimmer turns out to be a moose. Carl theorizes that wolves have chased it into the lake and with moose having notoriously poor eyesight, the animal does not know where the shore is.

Carl decides to throw an anchor rope around the moose's neck and slowly tow it to land. He and Art get the rope around the animal's neck and Carl starts the motor. The moose, however, takes off, away from the noise of the growling engine. Applying more power, Carl expects to force the moose to turn. Instead, as power is added, the moose's head is pulled under water, threatening to drown the animal.

The men decide to take the rope off and instead, with the skiff alongside the moose, Art puts his arms around the creature's neck and holds it against the boat while allowing it to swim. Carl uses the manual rudder to steer.

It takes hours but with the men changing off, they finally manage to guide the moose close to the beach. When its feet touch bottom, the moose cannot at first stand, as its legs are numb from the cold water it has been in for so long. The more temperate water near shore brings warmer blood to the moose and it gradually stumbles onto the beach, where it stands for some time, regaining its strength. Finally, the giant animal stumbles off into the woods behind Carl's house.

❦ CHAPTER 18 ❦

HERRING OR BLUEFIN?

George and wife Inga return from Duluth in 1922 and become significant participants in the resort.

Inga assumes responsibility for most of the accounting and bookkeeping functions and also plays the main role in recruiting and training waitresses. She continues a wifely tradition by lending a personal touch to the resort and begins some customs of her own. Apart from incorporating personal recipes into the Lutsen menu, she enjoys working around the resort. During Christmas season, she can often be seen making wreaths out of Prince's Pine branches. She particularly enjoys this work because she and her husband gather the pine together. Most years, Inga makes 20 to 25 wreaths and performs this labor of love for over 50 years.

Coffee is something else Inga enjoys making. A connoisseur, she takes special pride in her egg coffee.

At the same time, Inga maintains a professional but strict relationship with resort staff. She inspects staff uniforms each morning and enforces her work rules. Wait staff are not to write down food orders, regardless of the number of persons at a table. (Pity the poor waitress who serves Governor Youngdahl and his party of 13!) Wait staff are also to carry trays full of food at head level.

Staff is not always treated kindly by each other. Cooks, in particular, have a reputation for this, often keeping other staff waiting to eat until late in the day. Part of the reason for this, George believes, is that: *"It is difficult to find cooks who are not alcoholics."*

It is because of a cook, however, that Lutsen becomes known for a unique way of preparing herring. The resort obtains herring from a local fisherman named Reinert Reinertson who delivers the fish directly to the resort cook. One day the cook asks if Reinert could remove the skin before bringing up the fish. This is something unheard of but Reinert complies. Because some diners would turn up their noses at herring, the

69

dish is listed as "bluefin" and becomes a tremendous menu success.

A normal workday at the resort is 16 hours. For their labor, workers receive meals and a wage of $2.50 a day. If they do not live locally, they also receive lodging in "The Cottage" building, where they share a bathroom with up to seven other workers. The bathtub is used to wash uniforms.

Staff at the Lutsen Resort Dining Room

Despite the demanding work, the staff is a close-knit group. Some idea of the camaraderie they share can be gleaned from a ditty written by various staff years later and entitled "The Comedy of Waitresses:"

Lutsen
MINNESOTA

THE COMEDY OF WAITRESSES__LUTSEN, 1957

On the shore of Lake Superior
By the falls of Poplar River
Lay the famous all-year Lutsen
That to us will live forever.

Here the Swedes and Norse do gather
To vacation in our midst
While we who serve do humbly say,
"Eat your oats and fill up on hay!"

Everyday it seems to ve
That 6 a.m. does start the day.
The poor old house at the head of the hill
Shakes and shivers as it seems to say,
"CREW!!! DAYLIGHT IN THE SWAMP-
        UP AND AT 'EM JOANIE!!!"

From the ironing board flies uniforms
Round the corners sox and shoes
Somehow each one in his own way
Is prompt-though wondering who's whose.

Vel, vel goot morning Pat and Ellen,
Annie, Gert and others, too.
Then Liz at nine and all are here.
My, Du skal see travic folk
        (You should see this happy crew!)

Set tables, fold napkins, wipe silver and then
Stack dishes, cook coffee, again and again
Cut butter, get ice, squeeze oranges by hand
Then scrub off your mitts and gather your wits.

Convention Facilities FOR GROUPS UP TO 135

Settlers continue to move to Lutsen and Holst Hansen's store, now the Clearview store, becomes the first Lutsen business to open outside the resort.

In the spring of 1923, a bizarre event involving Carl Nelson's family unfolds. A 14-year-old runaway from a Wisconsin farm makes his way around the lakeshore until he comes to the Cross River. There, in order to avoid capture, he takes a boat and rows out onto Lake Superior until he is out of sight of land. That night, exhausted from hunger and fatigue, he rows back toward a light on shore. This turns out to be the Carl Nelson home. Carl is gone but his wife feeds and comforts the boy then calls the sheriff. The boy is taken to Grand Marais where he tells the sheriff he faces hardship in Wisconsin and does not want to go back. The juvenile is brought back to Carl's house where Mrs. Nelson promises a good home for him if Wisconsin authorities agree to let him stay. It is not known what ultimately becomes of the boy.

On a brighter note, CAA finishes building his hydroelectric plant and hosts a celebratory dinner at the resort. The News Herald of September 22 describes it:

"Guests saw the water-powered light and power plant that provides current for an up to date refrigerator plant, an electric range, and various other contrivances which provide convenience and save labor. Numerous improvements are being made each year and the original hotel is now much changed from what it was several years ago. The dining room is large and well ventilated with plenty of light. On the wall is the famous moose head, the largest ever taken in the state, according to Mr. Storey, taxidermist and sportsman of Duluth. It was shot by Mr. Nelson a couple of years ago. The new cottage on the bluff to the west of the main building was finished this year and has sleeping accommodations for 20. There are 85 bedrooms in all and the resort is popular. There were 48 for dinner Sunday."

The resort now has the only electricity between Two Harbors and Grand Marais.

The hydro-electric plant comprises a dam across the Poplar River, a flume, a cam stock set at an angle to turn a turbine, and belts to turn the generator. The resulting electricity powers lights, freezers, motors and pumps at the resort. In addition, the plant provides electricity to between 10 and 15 homes in the area that are lucky enough to be within the one-mile transmission limit. Transmission is limited because the current is direct and loses energy over a relatively short distance. Had the current been alternating, the whole town of Lutsen could easily have been supplied with electricity. As it is, all electrical appliances using the power have to have transformers on them or be made to use direct current. This is because the current in almost all cities is alternating and appliances are made there.

An interesting consequence of the plant results when CAA later considers obtaining even more power from further up the river. To this end, a three-foot diameter pipe is laid. The pipe is never completed to the headwaters of the river but it does extend far enough that when Highway 61 is built, an easement is required to build the Poplar River Bridge over the pipe. The pipe can still be seen from the bridge. Laying the pipe proves fortuitous because it allows the resort, years later, to serve liquor at both the main lodge and at the ski area. The liquor laws state that one license can cover multiple facilities only if they are contiguous. The pipe enables both facilities to meet this requirement and the license is approved by one vote.

On June 6, 1925, George Sr.'s wife Inga gives birth to a son, George Jr.

A few weeks later, on July 9, George Sr. attends the official opening of the Lake Superior International Highway in Two Harbors. The road runs for 168 miles, from Duluth to the Pigeon River on the Canadian border. The road helps keep the Lutsen resort busy, with about 100 guests staying there each day that summer. The road, however, will not be surfaced until the 1930s and Carl's son, Willard, notes that the road to Tofte is so bad that his family often drives to Grand Marais instead to do business.

After the road is built, CAA purchases a Buick truck and drives to Duluth once a week for food and other supplies. He also picks up mail for the Lutsen post office. Over the following years, every vehicle CAA buys is a Buick and he travels to the Buick factory in Flint, Michigan to negotiate a price and pick up the vehicle. It is characteristic of CAA to deal with the top people in an enterprise. In Minnesota, for example, he always directly approaches the governor or the commissioner of highways when he has an issue to raise.

The "Roaring Twenties" ends with a mixed outlook for the Nelsons and other North Shore residents.

The Cliff House, built in 1928, brings the total number of rooms at the resort to 85. There are more guests in the late 1920s than at any time until the townhouses are built. This is because, in those days, each room has three beds, a double and a single, yielding a capacity of 255 guests, (The main lodge has a capacity of 90 today). Also, in the old days, many more guests are hunters and fishermen who do not mind sleeping three to a room.

The Cliff House circa 1930

In 1929, a baby girl named Patti, who will have a significant impact on Lutsen, is born in Duluth to Tom and Bertha Eckel (nee Sivertson).

More ominously, major issues surface in the fishing industry. In October 1929, a special meeting of the North Shore Community Fishermen's Association passes a resolution forbidding the sale of fish caught outside the fishing season.

Not all North Shore fishermen agree with the resolution and a petition soon circulates, calling for opening the closed fishing season. In a portentous note for the industry, the News Herald speaks against the petition, noting on November 14 that:

"The decline in the supply of fish in the lake is no joke. It is a very real and very distressing thing."

As if this is not enough, the Great Depression is just beginning. However, despite the disastrous economy, or perhaps because of it, people are again vacationing close to home as they did during the war and the Lutsen resort does booming business throughout the summer of 1930.

The following year gets off to a literally rocky start when, in January, Gust, the Lutsen Postmaster, suffers a fractured arm from a boulder that crashes through the post office roof. The rock is from construction on Highway 61 above.

In 1932, CAA displays his famous "Champion of Champions" moose head at the World's Fair in Chicago where it is deemed a world record.

That same year, despite Minnesota's unemployment rate reaching 29%, CAA is optimistic about the future and tells the Herald he is going to improve the resort by providing:

- A swimming pool measuring 60 feet by 120 feet, that will necessitate moving several small buildings that will be used as part of new three-story hotel.

- A gravity pressure water system for hotel buildings and the pool, including a pipeline from the Poplar River to supply water.

- An airplane landing field, west of the main lodge.

- Additional hydro-electric power for lighting.

More immediately, the resort gets what the News Herald, in August, calls, *"...an artistic fountain, made from concrete and multi-colored sea shells of every description, with a four-way flow from four huge shells in a large center bowl. Shells also adorn a large arch, which covers all. The shells were collected last winter in Florida by CAA."*

The shells are actually collected by Anna. For years, in the resort lobby, she sells small animal figures made from pipe cleaners and shells.

The seashell fountain

Later, the Hansen store erects a copy of the fountain. Since demolished, two pieces of the structure remain, serving as bird feeders. They can be seen to the right of the store.

Meanwhile, the bad economic situation worsens. Ominously for Lutsen, three fourths of all tax delinquent property in Minnesota is in the northern part of the state.

In 1933 Cook County residents vote 145 to 42 to end prohibition and to bring back saloons. In the Lutsen precinct, the voting is 39 "wet" and only 4 "dry."

Interest in hay fever relief is renewed during 1935. In February, CAA is named to a statewide committee to; make the North Shore more favorable for hay fever sufferers, promote national interest in the region for those sufferers and bring recognition to the North Shore as a summer vacation center for hay fever sufferers. Plans include the eradication of weeds, particularly ragweed, along the North Shore. One problem is that there is so little ragweed, people cannot identify it easily. Accordingly, the committee recommends training people to identify and eliminate the weed. The promotional efforts are successful and that summer, hay fever sufferers are again flocking to Northern Minnesota.

The town of Lutsen, however, is not faring well and is dissolved on January 11, 1936. The dissolution occurs because a 1933 state law mandates dissolution for any town with a valuation under $50,000. Lutsen's valuation on December 10, 1935, is under $40,000. The reason is the economic depression and resultant delinquent tax crisis. The severity of the situation can be seen from Lutsen's receipt of only $646.66 for property taxes for all of 1935.

Oblivious to economic issues, in 1937, 12-year-old George Jr., and three friends go skiing. They practice their sport in a ravine wooded with birch trees and located on what is now Canyon Hole Number One of the Superior National Golf Course. This is George Jr.'s first downhill ski run and he has a wonderful afternoon, until his skis break. The thrill of skiing, however, remains with him throughout his life and will have an incredible impact on the entire North Shore, the State of Minnesota and the Upper Midwest region.

🐾 CHAPTER 19 🐾

BOBCAT ON MY BACK

Along with skiing, George Jr. pursues other, more serious winter pastimes. One of these is trapping. George Jr. and his cousin Clarence Elquist, often snowshoe all day to check trap lines they have laid. One such line is two to three miles long, starting at the Moose Road and running behind Moose Mountain. (Trap lines laid by adults are usually much longer, with shacks spaced along the line for overnight shelter.) The boys carry a gun for protection from wolves and bears, and a knapsack containing food. They neither have nor need a compass. Between 10 and 20 metal traps are attached to the line by chains. Although they might trap anything from a beaver to a lynx, marten, otter, mink, fox, wolf, muskrat or bear, the boys think it a good day if they catch a single weasel. They can sell a weasel pelt for $1 at Charlie Johnson's trading post in Grand Marais.

One bitterly cold Saturday, when the boys' feet are already frozen from trudging through deep snow, they find one trap missing. Following the tracks made by the trap and its chain, the boys finally come across a rare treasure, a hissing and spitting bobcat, ensnared between two small trees. The animal weighs about 20 pounds and its fur is worth up to $4 but only if they avoid shooting the creature, which would create a hole and greatly reduce the hide's value. The boys need to come up with another way to capture the unhappy and dangerous critter. They each wear leather thong shoelaces, which they remove and tie together. The resulting long string is tied into a square knot and lassoed around the cat's neck. The boys pull tightly on either end of the string. After much twitching and gasping, the cat is finally still.

Since Clarence is older and stronger, the animal is placed into his backpack and the boys are on their way, frozen feet forgotten at the prospect of looming wealth. It soon becomes evident, however, that the animal Clarence is carrying is a bobcat playing possum. Suddenly, the older boy lets out a piercing

scream that curdles George Jr.'s blood. Doubling over and
jumping up and down, Clarence begins yelling words his young
cousin has not heard before. All the while, Clarence tears at the
straps of his knapsack. It takes George Jr. a moment to realize
that their prize is not dead and, in an even fouler temper than
before, is now clawing and biting his way through the knapsack
and into Clarence's tender flesh. After what seems like a torture
session, Clarence is finally able to pull the knapsack off his
clawed and bloodied back. The youths retighten their makeshift
noose, this time pulling on it until their arms are too sore to
hang on anymore. Clarence is careful to make sure the cat is
definitely dead.

Back at the resort, the boys skin their prize in an outbuilding.
In a final swipe at its tormentors, the carcass gives off such a
putrid smell that George Jr. can recall the foul odor over 70
years later.

Since he lives on the shore of a large lake and on the bank of
a significant river, one might expect George Jr. to be an
accomplished swimmer. He is not. He does spend a lot of time
in the water with his friends. They particularly enjoy a swimming
hole in a Poplar River canyon where the bluffs rise to between
50 and 75 feet. Their favorite contest is to see who can go the
longest time without touching bottom. This must have been a
stubborn group of boys with not much else to do, because these
contests usually last about four hours. Consequently, George Jr.
becomes an excellent water treader but not a great swimmer.

When they tire of treading competitions, the boys enjoy
climbing the riverside cliffs and jumping into the water. One
day, cousin Clarence dislodges a rock that hits the trailing
George Jr. full in the face, knocking him into the river, far
below. Luckily, he is not seriously injured. A measure of the
risks accepted at the time can be gauged from the reaction of
George Jr.'s mother when he shows up back at Lutsen.
Although George Jr. can tell that she is scared by his appearance
and narrow escape, she has only two words for him: *"Be
sensible."*

Another woman who perhaps questions the amount of sense
George Jr. has, is one of his schoolteachers. Located on the

Caribou Lake Road in a building that now houses the Lutsen
Fire Department, the "new" Lutsen School has two rooms
downstairs and two up. (Originally, enrollment is small enough
that two female teachers lived downstairs and have a kitchen.) In
George Jr.'s schooldays, total enrollment is still less than 50
students and two teachers conduct 15-minute classes to grades
one through eight. George Jr. shares classes with two other
students. The amount of sense George Jr. possesses is
questioned by Miss England, a teacher who says more than
once, *"I wonder what will become of you, George Nelson."*

George Jr. never figures out if his teacher thinks him a genius
or an idiot.

🐾 CHAPTER 20 🐾

A ROYALE UPBRINGING

There is at least one young lady who thinks George Jr. is quite sensible. Her name is Patti Eckel and it is she who was born in Duluth back in 1929. Her father is from Detroit and becomes a keeper at the Rock of Ages lighthouse on Isle Royale. Standing 130 feet tall, with walls four and a half feet thick at the base to withstand storm waves that can crash 30 feet up the tower, the lighthouse warns of a reef three miles west of the island. Patti's father is one of four keepers manning the light, which burns from dusk to dawn and is rotated by hand cranking every hour. In cold, stormy weather, keepers walk on the outer tower to keep the glass free of snow and ice. To maintain visibility, every day the light must be cleaned of soot from the illuminating kerosene lamp. The penalty for failing to perform these duties is immediate dismissal and loss of all pension rights, not to mention great dishonor. No wonder the Rock is considered a punishing assignment.

As he tends the light, Patti's father can see innumerable large fish swimming among the rocks in the clear water below. He thinks it must be easier to catch such fish than be a lighthouse keeper, so he borrows a net from an Isle Royale fisherman named Sivertson. This proves fortuitous in two respects. First, spreading the net around the dock by his lighthouse does indeed allow him to catch many fish, which leads him to become a successful commercial fisherman. Second, and more importantly, he meets Sivertson's daughter who becomes his wife and the mother of Patti.

Patti's youth is very different from that of George Jr. The Eckel summer shack on Isle Royale has no running water and utilizes an outhouse. Children's activities on the island include rowing around miles of island shoreline and to other islands with no life preservers. There is also swimming, although, according to one participant, this is more of an endurance test than a good time. In a 1986 interview about growing up on Isle Royale, one island boy says, *"If you couldn't stay in the water for at least an hour, you were a sissy. Kids living on the island in those days would often emerge from the water purple and shaking badly. Until I reached adulthood, I thought you were supposed to suffer from hypothermia every time you went swimming. I never realized there was such a thing as a warm lake."*

One cold thing the island kids crave is ice cream. There is no ice cream store, so the delicacy is brought from the mainland, packed in salt. Another treat Patti and her brothers are allowed is a case of pop. This is to last all summer but Patti's brothers invariably drink their share after only a few weeks. They then barter with Patti for some of hers, offering one stick of gum from the single pack each child is granted for the year. Other treats the island kids look forward to are Mrs. Barnum's campfires and marshmallow roasts, and Grandma Sivertson's fresh-baked rye bread, which can be smelled all over the island.

When Patti is 10, her mother dies and Patti takes on more mature responsibilities within the family. Her father eventually remarries and at age 17, Patti leaves Isle Royale to live and work in Grand Marais. She has always been an outstanding student, finishing top of her class at Cook County High School. The loss of her mother and her poor childhood haunt Patti nonetheless. One Home Economics assignment is to sew a pinafore apron. With no sewing machine and no mother to guide her, Patti does not receive a perfect score for the class. This imagined failure makes her determined that her own children will never endure the same thing and one of her first purchases after her marriage is a sewing machine.

Outside school, Patti, like George Jr., has chores. Her family rents out some rooms and she does laundry and cleans the rooms. In her mid-teens, Patti also takes a summer job as a telephone operator. She prefers working the night shift so she can enjoy her beloved outdoors during the day. One of her favorite outdoor activities is hunting partridge. She is a good shot, using a rifle instead of a shotgun, because *"...you have to hit the head."*

Robert Mc Dowell

Successful partridge hunt

Another pastime Patti enjoys is roller-skating at the old rink on Highway 7. She is not as good at that as she is at shooting and would *"...hit the wall lots..."*

83

🐾 CHAPTER 21 🐾

LIGHT BEFORE THE STORM

By 1938, Lutsen is making a comeback. In May, the Lutsen Evangelical Lutheran Church is dedicated. Formerly the Hebron Lutheran Building in Grand Marais, the building is purchased from the Swedish Augustana Synod, moved to Lutsen, and placed on land donated by Mr. and Mrs. Holst Hansen.

One month later, the News Herald reports another innovative business venture being undertaken in Lutsen:

"A new and interesting sport is being developed at Lutsen resort according to the management. A trap and skeet shoot will be held there beginning Sunday morning at 10 o'clock. The sport will be continued throughout the summer as a pastime for the summer guests staying there and for any local people interested. This is one of the sports being developed here to keep the tourist busy when the fish refuse to bite."

The shooting range is across Highway 61 from the resort, where Hole Number One of the Superior National Golf Course is now located.

The success of Lutsen sometimes makes its residents feel like they are living in crowded conditions and in November, at least one resident complains, *"Lutsen is once again a small town alive with tourists but hunting this season will be a real sport as the woods are so noisy that those who get deer will deserve them."*

Another measure of the town's success is the arrival of electricity for all residents. This occurs as part of President Roosevelt's *"...light bulb in every barn"* campaign. In August of 1940, the News Herald's Lutsen correspondent reports that: *"The new electrical power line at Lutsen is materializing. Poles are up and engine installed so we are looking forward to completion of wiring so we can enjoy modern lighting."*

In February of 1941, all of Lutsen finally has modern lighting.

That CAA electrified his resort and some homes in town almost 20 years earlier underscores what a pioneer and innovator he is. With the arrival of electricity from the power company, the resort has no need for its hydroelectric plant and it shuts down.

Lutsen and other North Shore communities have advanced in other ways. Instead of steamboats coming to pick up fish as weather permits, or instead of spending days transporting their fish to Duluth themselves, fishermen along the shore can now catch fish early in the morning and have them iced and ready for pick up by truck in the afternoon. The trucks take the fish to Duluth, where they are re-iced and put on a train. The next morning the fish are being sold at fish markets as far away as Chicago.

Also in February, George Sr. is elected President of the Grand Marais Chamber of Commerce. The Chamber's main purpose is to encourage tourism along the North Shore. George demonstrates a personal and passionate approach to the job that is acknowledged when the News Herald states, *"If there is a big influx of Iowa people from the Des Moines area this summer, it will probably be due in great part to the salesmanship of George Nelson."*

George also demonstrates some of his inherited innovative thinking when, in July, the Chamber of Commerce shows movies in the streets of Grand Marais *"...with the purpose of entertaining, as well as informing the tourists where to go and how to spend their vacation days."*

With World War II looming, George focuses on the effect of the war on travel and tourism. In November, he assures his colleagues that *"...regardless of the concentrated war effort, a great number of fishermen and vacationists will be seeking accommodations this summer. To prove this, we secured the greatest number of prospective listings ever..."*

The News Herald indicates that the nation's leaders agree with George. The paper quotes these leaders as saying:

"Time must be taken for rest in order that the vacationists can return to their jobs with new life and vigor."

George does not realize that, while his prediction is accurate, he and his family will not be on the North Shore for most of the war years and ongoing operation of the Lutsen resort will depend on others.

❧ CHAPTER 22 ❧

FROM FINE DINING TO MESS HALL

When the U.S. enters the war, Walt Williams, the man who fly fished for bass, tells George Sr. of an opportunity to serve his country. Williams is a Chicago restaurateur and food service manager and he advises George that the army is looking for leading civilians in the food industry, men such as George, with years of experience, who can help make food service a vital force in the war effort. Williams suggests that George and his wife consider contracting to serve food to munitions workers. George decides this would be a patriotic thing to do and is assigned to the Sangamon Ordnance Plant in Illinois to begin operations. Wife Inga, daughter Norrine and son George Jr. join him later.

Used to serving less than 100 people at a time, George now faces a Herculean task that he outlines in a July 1943 letter to the News Herald: *"We have had a busy past week ... They have plants that employ up to forty thousand. That's a real feeding job. We are feeding almost ten thousand daily now, so it's quite a plant. We have eleven cafeterias but the cooking is all done in one and food is distributed around to the various cafeterias, which makes it a difficult job."*

Pickup trucks transport the food between cafeterias scattered over several square miles. The food is kept hot in carts.

George works at the Sangamon plant until August 1945. At about that time, a report by the Army Quartermaster's Food Service Program indirectly notes his significant contribution: *"The Office of the Quartermaster General, as staff agency of the Army Service Forces, organized a Food Service Program which went into effect on 31 July, 1943. Since that time, tremendous strides have been made in food service. Soldiers today are much better fed. Waste has been reduced at least fifty per cent. Hundreds of progressive ideas have been put into effect and have saved millions of dollars."*

During George's time in Illinois, Inga returns to Lutsen to run the resort, with help from Clara Moen, a longtime employee. This is a busy time, because vacationers are again limited to staying near home and with gasoline rationing, many guests come by bus. Sinclair Lewis, on his way to Canada, is the first visitor to register when the resort opens on June 15, 1944. Food rationing exacerbates problems because rations are based on the previous year's occupancy, which was lower than is currently being experienced. Consequently, supplies of some rationed items are insufficient for the many guests.

The war also casts a literal shadow over Lutsen. Large bomber planes use points along the shoreline for target practice, flying low, diving and shooting. After they leave, 50-caliber shells can be found in ditches and on beaches. On other days, squadrons of planes appear a mile high, making their way across Lake Superior, bound for a refueling stop in Canada before heading on to join the battle in Europe.

❦ CHAPTER 23 ❦

EVERYBODY GOES INTO THE INFANTRY

Meanwhile, George Jr. finishes high school in Decatur but asks to graduate from Grand Marais High School. This is agreed and he graduates at age 18. He has known since Pearl Harbor that he will be directly involved in the war. On that day of infamy, he is just 16 and driving in the backcountry with a friend when they hear on the radio that Pearl Harbor has been bombed. *"We'll be in that,"* George Jr. says. *"We'll be in that for sure, if it lasts more than two years."* In October 1943, he sets off to join the army.

George Jr. has seen Pathe newsreels in theaters report that the U.S. Army is forming a mountain infantry division and is looking for a few good men. Volunteers must meet two requirements: they must be used to cold weather and, since this is an elite unit, applicants must produce three letters of recommendation. George Jr. obtains his letters and is duly qualified. He is inducted into the military at Camp Grant, Illinois and assigned to Camp Hale, Colorado. On the train to Denver, George Jr.'s sheltered life on the North Shore causes him some discomfort when he has to share a carriage bunk with another guy.

Further horrors await him on the Trailways bus to Camp Hale. The rear wheels of the bus are 15 feet from the back of the bus where George Jr. sits. When the bus goes over the 12,500 feet Loveland Pass, it cannot make one of the turns and has to back up, putting its rear wheels at the edge of a cliff. This leaves George Jr. hanging over the edge of the mountain. His belly flutters increase when he looks down and sees several vehicle hulks far below.

On arrival at the Camp Hale front gate, George Jr. checks in with the adjutant, who asks, *"What kind of a unit do you want to go into?"*

"Which one skis most?" George Jr. responds.

The adjutant smiles. *"Infantry,"* he replies, and then adds, *"Everybody asks that, and everybody goes into the infantry."*

Later, George Jr. admits that he did not know there was a
transportation unit, a medical unit and a supply unit. Had he
known, he says he would have been smart and said he knew how
to drive a jeep. That way, he thought he would get to drive an
officer around. As he put it years later, *"I learned well, but I
learned late."*

And so, George Jr. becomes a ski trooper in the 10th
Mountain Division. For an unrelenting 18 months he trains in
rock climbing, snowshoeing, and skiing, He learns survival
techniques by enduring 20 continuous days in sub-zero
temperatures. The trainees are not above trying to make things a
little easier and George Jr. notes, *"They used to fill our packs to
weigh 90 pounds. We would cheat and put toilet paper in them,
so they looked big. That was soon figured out. We trained with
heavy, heavy packs."*

During his training, George Jr. conceives the idea of opening
a ski area at Lutsen, thereby converting his family's summer-only
resort into a year round operation. He knows the Sawtooth
Mountains, paralleling Lake Superior about two miles inland,
have favorable conditions for winter sports, including the
greatest vertical drop and length in the upper Midwest.

After a year and a half of training and waiting for action,
George Jr.'s unit gets its orders to move out in June of 1944. No
one knows where they are headed but they take their heavy
winter clothes. This is unfortunate, because the unit is sent to
Camp Swift, near Austin, Texas. Perhaps this is to confuse the
enemy but it is far more bewildering to the troops to get off a
train in thick, woolen clothes and step into temperatures
hovering around 100 degrees.

🐾 CHAPTER 24 🐾

BETTER LUCKY THAN SMART

George Jr. finally sees combat in the Apennine Mountains of Northern Italy from January 1945 until the end of the war in May. The ski troops have a high casualty rate but George Jr. is not injured, although not from lack of exposure to danger. Here is his recollection of a particularly risky operation:

"February 19, 1944 Italy - Combat.

Finally, we are attacking, picking our way up Mount Belvedere. It is close to midnight and very dark but no light of any kind is allowed. We also have no ammunition in our rifles because an accidental discharge will alert the enemy. Our orders are to take no prisoners. I do not like that.

I also do not like knowing there are trip wires strung between the trees and if I trip one... well, I do not want to be the first guy to call for a medic. Soon enough, there is an explosion and somebody does call for a medic. Shortly after, the same thing happens. This alerts the enemy and mortar shells and 88's [88 mm artillery shells] begin to rain down on us. I can tell they are mostly mortars because, in battle, one quickly learns the physics of war: 88's have a flat trajectory while mortar shells fall more vertically.

The steep mountainside is heavily wooded and we advance slowly. As we near the top, machine guns open fire on us. They are far enough away that, although we can see their tracers coming, they burn out before reaching us. In between each tracer are four bullets that cannot be seen. The mortars and the 88's are still falling around us.

Another fellow and I are carrying heavy packs full of ammunition and grenades. I also have a Browning automatic rifle, which is heavier than a standard-issue. I tell the guy we need to run to get out of this. It is hard to believe that with all our gear, we can run up a mountain in the dark. I ask myself how far we should run and decide to keep going until I stop hearing bullets hitting around me. I feel my heart rising in my throat. We make it beyond the machine gun fire but when I turn around, the guy is not there. There are other guys who had been behind him but he is gone, just disappeared.

The following morning I am on top of a ridge and I do something stupid. I start walking. I don't know why. I hear a buzz, buzz, buzz and wonder if there are hornets around. Then, cold realization hits me – there would not be hornets in February with snow on the ground! Looking down, I see the grass breaking in front of my knees. To an infantry soldier in combat, the ground is his best friend. To be dug into it is best and to be lying on it is next best. To be standing on it, as I am, is really bad.

Throwing myself down, I look to see where these things are coming from. I glimpse a black circle that passes over my shoulder. It is an "88" coming in. If I had been further along it would have blown my head off. It lands about 50 feet beyond me."

After 11 days and 10 nights on the mountain, George Jr. bears the marks of war but no physical scars:

"My combat pants have fourteen holes, with two in each pocket and two in the crotch, yet I am uninjured. With so many people killed and wounded all around me, it's hard to believe I am so lucky."

Remember that when he reported to Camp Hale and realized he could have signed up to be a driver, George Jr. noted that he learned well but learned late. Fortunately, George Jr. does not learn late in combat. Among the things he and his buddies find out are:

"If you can survive the first week, you have a good chance of surviving the second. If you accomplish that, you are an old-timer with a chance of making it for a while. As you become more seasoned, you develop a survival instinct. You get your mind in gear and develop a number of faculties. One is mind control. You keep telling yourself to do your job and support your buddies. You do not want to be a coward or make a mistake. You become nervous and start analyzing everything, even how to lie in a foxhole. You try to figure out the best way to position your knees. One way may be more comfortable but

might expose you more to shrapnel. That leads you to think about where shrapnel is likely to land, and so on. If you can get a week or two of experience, you start to know things. Once your mind knows what to do, your body must obey immediately and respond correctly. You will make mistakes but must avoid critical ones. They say it is better to be lucky than smart and I believe that but I think you can position yourself to be lucky. If you position yourself not to be lucky, you will not be lucky. You have to position yourself and I was lucky."

In between risk analysis and positioning himself to be lucky, George Jr. has time to marvel at the absurdities of war:

"We have a toothbrush to clean our guns but not for our teeth. So, you use one toothbrush for both, with no toothpaste, of course."

There are also chilling discoveries in the efficient use of everyday items:

"I can't remember having a blanket but I am issued a mattress cover. It is for putting a body in. Everybody has a mattress cover..."

George Jr.'s division is at the front for 110 days and has the most casualties per day of any division of the U.S. Army in Italy. Of 7,000 infantry from his division who served at the front, 998 are killed, with 3,800 wounded. Overall, the division suffers about a 70% casualty rate.

On an even more personal level, George Jr.'s squad of 12 men suffers three killed and four wounded.

George Jr. becomes his squad's eighth casualty when he contracts pneumonia. Classified as walking wounded, he leaves the front to walk back to the field hospital. Along the way, he witnesses a horrific scene:

"It is an ugly, ugly walk. I learn what the death squad is. I almost do not want to know. The death squad comes through after a battle and picks up the dead from both sides, puts the bodies in bags and hauls the corpses out of there. All armies do this. They get the dead out so it is not mentally defeating for troops to go back to these fields."

George Jr. is hospitalized on April 12, 1945, the day President Roosevelt dies. The war ends a few weeks later.

The skis George Jr. used during the war are on display at the Cross River Heritage Center in Schroeder.

🐾 CHAPTER 25 🐾

END OF AN ERA

B ack in Minnesota, George Sr. purchases the resort from CAA in May, 1945. The News Herald reports, *"The new owners are not yet sure what will be done in the way of operating the resort this summer, because of their work at Decatur."*

One thing the new owners wonder about is the impact of a potential major change to the Superior lakeshore. Under the Federal River and Harbor Act, Lutsen is identified as the site of a proposed refuge harbor. The proposal includes two converging breakwaters with a 60 feet wide entrance and three channels with depths of six, eight, and twelve feet. However, nothing more will be heard about this project until 1960.

In August of 1945, the Nelson family is reunited at Lutsen. George Sr., Inga and Norrine come from Illinois and George Jr. is in from Italy. One change the young soldier notices is that the Lutsen post office is no longer located on the resort grounds. Because there are few long-term guests at the resort during the war, the post office moves to the Lockport Store and Jessie Bally becomes Post Master. The post office moves to its present location after the war.

In February 1946, George Jr., discharged from the army, enrolls at Michigan State University to study Hotel Administration. He craves home cooking when he sees the Lutsen resort featured in the October issue of the Ford Motor Company magazine "Ford Times." The "Famous Recipes of Famous Taverns" article includes the recipe for his mother's Swedish rye bread, which is still available today.

Young George Jr.'s recollections of his grandmother are even more poignant when she dies of a heart attack on December 26, 1947. In its obituary of January 1, 1948, the News Herald notes:

"Mrs. Charles AA Nelson, 84, died of a heart attack at her daughter's house in Lutsen where she had been staying. She had a previous heart attack earlier in the month but had recovered sufficiently to have Christmas dinner with the family. Until about

3 years ago, Mrs. Nelson was a genial hostess while also bringing up her four sons and three daughters. Surviving her are her husband, sons, Carl, Edward, George and Oscar all of Lutsen and daughters Ida, Hilda and Elsie, along with 26 grandchildren and 25 great grandchildren."

The passing of Anna Matilda presages some rough years ahead for the Nelson family. Just 16 days after his wife's death, CAA dies on January 11, 1948. His obituary reads:

"CAA Nelson, 84, Pioneer Resorter, dies at Lutsen

CAA Nelson, 84, died at the home of his daughter at Lutsen. He had been in poor health for some time. The death of his wife occurred just 16 days previously.

Known primarily as the man who originated the resort business in the state, he was also a pioneer leader in many other ways.

Born April 27, 1863, in Morchiping Sweden, son of Nels Olson and Margaret Samuelson Olson. He received his early education in Sweden and come to the U.S. in 1883, going first to Minneapolis where he worked as a carpenter and mason for about two years. He was captain of a small tug operating up the North Shore for a commercial fish company. About this time, he became interested in taking a homestead on the North Shore. His claim was at first challenged by another pioneer, but the Duluth land office found his application valid. He married Anna Matilda Peterson in Duluth. The next year on June 30, they and son Carl came to the homestead at the Poplar River where they have remained since. It was here that members of the Duluth Board of Trade visited a year or so later which marked the beginning of his now famous resort endeavors.

People came by boat to stay part of the summer or to hunt moose at Camp Nelson, the lodge on the Moose Road, which was established in 1900 and operated for 25 years.

His activities during the first 30 years overlapped considerably. He conducted logging operations: was a commercial fisherman: conducted a general store: was Lutsen postmaster and served as county commissioner: chairman of Lutsen town board and school board as well as in 1890 enumerator for census for the western half of the County. He was a member of the Duluth and Grand Marais chambers of commerce and a life member of the Duluth Masonic order.

Four sons, 3 daughters: 26 grandchildren: 25 great grandchildren survive. Also mourning is Clara Moen who has long been in the employ of the Nelsons, both at Lutsen and when they made their annual winter trips to Florida."

Among CAA's last words to his grandson, George Jr., are, *"Lutsen has been good to the Nelsons, and the Nelsons must be good to Lutsen."* These words have a profound effect on young George Jr.

So ends an era. A young Swedish farmhand realized his dream of seeing America and brought his family to share its opportunities. CAA took advantage of and shared the bounty he discovered. Now his body is literally part of his new land. His town, resort, cemetery and grave will forever recall the boy who, born in the old world, shaped a new one.

🐾 CHAPTER 26 🐾

FIRE AND DESTRUCTION

Six months after CAA's death, Lutsen Resort suffers another terrible blow. The News Herald of June 10, 1948 reports the event:

"Lutsen Resort suffers loss by fire

Lutsen Resort suffered a major loss by fire yesterday morning when the 20-room dormitory on the hill (known as the "Old 20") was completely destroyed. It burned so fiercely and quickly that nothing was saved. It had just been made ready for the summer season.

Smoke was noticed about 8 o'clock but by the time the owners reached the scene it was too far along to save the furniture. The origin of the fire is unknown, but the Nelsons believe it started at the kerosene hot water heater located in the center of the one story building. A maid had lit the heater 20 minutes prior to the blaze. It started so fast they believe it was an explosion. The property was only partially insured. Although there was no one in the building yesterday, two large groups had been housed there several days ago to officially open the season at the resort. The 32-room dormitory across the road was endangered by sparks but since there was no wind the flames shot up instead of toward the building."

A few days after the fire, George Jr. arrives home from college to help his parents. He stays a year before going back to finish his studies.

July 29 is an important day for the whole North Shore region and indeed, for Minnesota. The resort hosts a celebration of "Minnesota's Great Wilderness Project." Governor Luther Youngdahl and many of Minnesota's foremost public officials and citizens attend. George Sr. uses the occasion to announce that Lutsen will soon open Minnesota's first winter sports resort.

This event produces a blizzard of publicity for the North Shore in general and Lutsen in particular. Veteran journalists covering the event provide the area with more newspaper and radio publicity than ever before. Day after day, front-page articles concerning the area appear in leading newspapers of the Midwest. National press coverage follows. NBC radio carries a one-hour program from the resort, telling the world of the natural beauties, attractions and health-giving climate of the area. The North Shore and Lutsen are on the map and George Sr. spares no expense to impress important guests.

In late September, the resort hosts 250 attendees at a Rotarian Convention. The News Herald reports that:

"For these conventions, George Nelson, proprietor of the resort, imports a specialty chef from Duluth who is a master in ice carvings. For this event, he fashioned a beautiful ice vase, filled with flowers."

Things are definitely looking up when disaster strikes again on October 18. The News Herald reports the tragedy on October 21:

"Lutsen Resort Destroyed by Fire Early Monday morning
Loss Valued at $200,000. Origin of Blaze unknown. No One Hurt.

A fire of unknown origin leveled historic Lutsen Resort early Monday morning when the main lodge, the laundry building and the old store building that had been converted into a dormitory for the help, fountain service and store room for supplies burned to the ground.

The fire was discovered about 4 a.m. by Mrs. Carl Carlson who awakened when she heard a noise from the kitchen. Her first thought was that her aunt, Mrs. J. Toftey whom she was caring for, had tumbled from the bed. When she reached her bed, she noticed smoke issuing into the room and immediately roused the resort owners, Mr. and Mrs. George Nelson and Miss Clara Moen, clerk and secretary at the resort, who were asleep on the second floor.

While Mr. Nelson tried to get into the kitchen, Mrs. Nelson helped Mrs. Carlson get the former's mother into a wheelchair. Mr. Nelson found the kitchen all ablaze and filled with so much smoke he could not enter. Mrs. Carlson took Mrs. Toftey to the dormitory on the hill.

Meantime, there was a scurry to get the help aroused in the other building. So quickly did the building burn that there was no time to save a thing.

Mr. Nelson estimates the loss at about $200,000, some of which was included in new installations such as a new furnace just being installed, a new refrigeration system in the kitchen, a new washer in the laundry and 3 new picture windows in the lounge, to mention a few. Most of the loss, which was keenly felt, was embodied in historic relics collected over a space of 40 or 50 years.

Generally known as the first resort in Minnesota, the lodge was originated by Mr. Nelson's father, CAA, back in the old moose hunting days at the turn of the century. People came by boat from Duluth and spent their vacations at the resort. From there, they made trips inland for hunting and fishing.

Too stunned to make immediate plans, the Nelsons are marking time until a decision can be made. Only this spring, they lost one of the dormitories, which in itself was a heavy loss. Only one dormitory, 3 cabins and the filling station remain of the famous resort."

There is speculation that the blaze began as a grease fire in the kitchen but this is never confirmed.

🐾 CHAPTER 27 🐾

A DREAM COME TRUE

George Jr. has imagined a ski resort at Lutsen since his army training days in Colorado. As part of his planning, he visits Minnesota's first ski lift, built on a bluff near Shakopee. After that trip, George Jr. gathers some Sun Valley ski fans at a Minneapolis hotel to tell them he is considering installing Minnesota's second uphill lift at Lutsen. *"You're crazy,"* they tell him. *"It's too cold and too remote."* George Sr. is more supportive of his son's idea. He loves skiing, having learned the sport at the Telemark resort in Wisconsin and will enjoy it until age 85, when his eyesight deteriorates. Father and son have been working on a ski hill for many months. Now they must rebuild the resort. A family council is held to decide how to proceed.

The decision is to seize the opportunity to make the resort bigger and better than ever by completing the ski slope while rebuilding the main resort.

As a first step in this latter task, George Sr. establishes a lumber camp at Lake Agnes. A mill is built to cut the timber and a diesel engine is installed to run the logging equipment. The main lodge is rebuilt using timber from this operation, including rare white pine. The logs are skidded using a tractor and the timber is trucked to the resort using a Bobcat truck. George Jr., who often operates this vehicle, remembers that sometimes the load would be too heavy, causing the Bobcat's front wheels to rise like the front legs of a bucking bronco. This problem is addressed by cantilevering a heavy log over the hood of the bobcat and chaining it down. This resolves the balance issue but makes for a spine-tingling ride downhill from Lake Agnes to the resort, since the heavy front weight makes it impossible to steer without judicious application of the brakes.

Working conditions are difficult. George Jr. recalls it being so cold one day that when his uncle Oscar goes to change the oil in the Bobcat, he cannot get oil to pour from the can. Thinking only the top layer of oil is frozen, Oscar cuts into the can. By the time he finishes, the complete quart of oil sits solid outside the can and is still there the next morning.

Originally, the ski area is to be built on Moose Mountain. This area was purchased by the Nelsons for payment of taxes owed since the 1890s. High rock ledges and a lack of snow to cover boulders, however, make it an unusable location.

The eventual and current location is chosen for several reasons. First, it is inland, which allows relatively warm, moist air from Lake Superior to cool enough so that snow on the ski slopes will not melt. Second, the location allows for a ski run of over 6,000 feet. Third, the Poplar River ravine provides an extra 200 feet of slope with a 630 feet vertical drop. This is the highest vertical drop between the Appalachians and the Rockies. Finally, the location allows access to hundreds of miles of cross-country skiing.

The ski area is designed and built by George Jr. and his father. This includes runs, ski lifts and access roads. George Sr. creates a snow-packing vehicle by bolting two by four pieces of lumber to the treads of a tractor. This allows packing of a seven to eight feet wide path. Trees are manually felled with a crosscut saw and cut as close to the ground as possible. The resultant stumps, usually about an inch high, are packed over with snow. This leaves the root structure intact in the soil, preventing erosion. A resort employee named Harry performs most of this packing, carrying snow in a bushel basket and using a shovel to tamp down the snow. This also has to be done if bare spots develop on the slopes during ski season. In recognition of Harry's backbreaking labor, the first slope completed is named Hari Kari, which suggests a suicide run and is a play on Harry's basket carrying. The other slope, for beginners, is named Chickadee.

On December 10, 1948, the News Herald reports that:

"The Lutsen Resort Ski area with tow at Lutsen is just about complete and all that is lacking at this writing is a bit more snow. This ski resort is located north of the Lutsen resort site on a north slope with majestic scenery. The tow will take the skier up the steep incline and put him at the top of a grand runway that will test anyone's skill. There will be less abrupt hills where

*beginners can try out their ski legs and a series of ski lessons will
be given to those who wish to enroll. Two skiways are in this
year and more are planned for later. The power for the tow will
come from the gasoline engine perched on the very top of the
hill. This has already been installed and most of the towline is
in.*

*At the bottom of the tow, a 24 x 40 warming house is being
completed. One wall of this house is practically all windows to
afford a good view of the ski run. George Nelson, owner of the
ski area, stated yesterday that he believes most of the activity on
the hill will be on weekends but he will keep the place open
daily if business warrants. Hot coffee will be served at the
warming house."*

The ski hill officially opens for business on Sunday,
December 19. Everyone is invited to bring skis, try out the new
tow, and ski for free. The idea is to get local folks interested in
the sport and the Nelsons feel vindicated when they find
themselves hosting a large crowd. Many come as spectators only
but a good number bring skis, select the hill best suited to their
abilities and try out the slopes. Many report the greatest thrill as
being pulled uphill by the new powered tow. They do not mind
that they often cannot outlast the hill on the way down.
Spectators, many of whom watch from the warming house on
top of the first hill, cheer each skier who gracefully completes a
run and laugh heartily when there is a spectacular spill. It is
good-natured and by all accounts, most people have the time of
their lives.

Thus does Lutsen become the first Minnesota resort to offer
skiing, although during that first year the slopes are only open on
weekends. Nonetheless, one of the most successful recreational
developments in the Midwest and a furnace that will fuel the
North Shore economy for years to come, is born.

The birth, however, is not without complications. With the
Lutsen resort out of commission following the fire a few months
before, housing is needed for skiers from outside the area. This
is an important consideration since the Lutsen ski population
comes from further away than other any other major ski area.

The Nelsons ask anyone with accommodations available to contact them.

A secondary problem relates to the foibles of Mother Nature. It is difficult to collect and retain snow on the slopes. East winds bring snow but Northwest winds blow it away. It is not until after the first year of operation that snow fences are built to hold the snow in place. The fences, constructed from birch trunks and wire, can be moved to different areas to create drifts. Spruce trees are planted to help retain snow. These steps work well but perfect skiing conditions are still beyond control. Ideally, snow will fall on Monday, Tuesday and Wednesday so the slopes have a good snowpack. Snow, however, is not wanted on Thursdays, Fridays or Saturdays because that makes it difficult for skiers to travel to the slopes.

Among those early ski crowds are Patti and a group of friends, enjoying Christmas vacation. Patti cannot ski but a mutual friend introduces her to George Jr. She returns several times to ski, allowing George Jr. to teach her. Eventually, she goes to his house for dinner. After that, some of her time with George Jr. is spent packing snow on the wind-blown ski slopes.

The New Year sees expansion of the infant ski resort with another slope opening. It is named Koo Koo because people think it is "cuckoo" to build such a slope, which is an even more challenging run than Hari Kari.

Koo Koo and Chickadee are connected to the same engine for power to their rope tows. This seems like an efficient use of resources but a huge disadvantage is quickly discovered when the engine malfunctions and both slopes are unusable.

One early skier who encounters this problem is George Hovland, who will go on to become an Olympic Nordic skier in the 1950s. George tells of his first Lutsen skiing experience:

"My first skiing experience at Lutsen was in 1948. I was in a group of four University of Minnesota ski club members on our way from Minneapolis to Mount McKay - now Thunder Bay - Canada. As we drove past the Lutsen resort, we noticed a board nailed to a tree on the North side of Highway 61 where a side road went up a hill. Hand-painted on the sign in red letters were

the words "Ski Tow." The letters looked like they had been written with a stick. One of us yelled, "Stop! Let's go up!"

Reaching the end of the side road, we found ourselves in front of a building that looked like a small double car garage. There were two cleared slopes covered with untracked snow flanking a rope tow. We went into the building, which was actually the chalet, to find three men, who I later learned were George Nelson Sr., George Jr. and his uncle Oscar. They were warming themselves around a barrel stove. Before we could ask, one of the Georges said, "We are not open and the tow is not running."

We learned this was a new slope named Koo Koo and asked if we could walk up it and ski. They looked at each other as though we were nuts and but finally said "OK."

We grabbed our skis and started walking up the towline in about 18 inches of new, untouched powder. Reaching the top of the slope, we lined up and went down side-by-side, leaving four parallel tracks. It was not a fast trip in the soft deep snow.

Being competitive, I led with one ski pushed forward to gain bragging rights as the first one to ski down this new hill.

We went into the chalet to thank the men. Oscar looked at us and scratching his head, said in a strong Swedish accent, "I ain't never seen nuttin like dat before, I vouldn't even ride a pole down that hill!" He was referring to an old style of skiing with a long pole held between the legs to control speed and direction.

That was my first of many visits to Lutsen's ski slopes."

One of those visits would lead George to an incredible opportunity:

"It was around November of 1950. The snow was good, and we were bombing the speed bumps, showing off for the crowd sitting on the chalet deck. We were fearless and the way the run was profiled, we would come straight down, bouncing off the bumps at full speed and shoot into the sharp transition at the bottom, then up the slope toward the deck, stopping short and showering snow on the onlookers.

During a break, I went into the chalet and was confronted by a middle-aged man in ski gear who screamed of wealth, power and sophistication. He looked at me and said in a tone that was warm but demanding, "Where the hell did you learn to ski like that?"

"I... I... I... here, just here sir."

"You telling me you've never skied out West?"

"N...n...n...no sir."

"How would you like to try to make the Olympic Team, go train with the Alpine team members in Sun Valley?"

I was almost speechless but managed to get out that I would like that but I would be trying out for the Cross Country team, not Downhill.

He looked puzzled but finally said that was OK because the U.S. team had hired a Swedish cross-country coach who lived in Sun Valley and I could train with him. He pulled out his business card and said, "Be in my office Monday morning if you are interested."

I found his office near the top of the tallest building in downtown Minneapolis. The office had an imposing 12-feet high, ornate wooden door. I entered and, presenting the business card to a secretary, introduced myself.

The secretary opened another office door and whispered my name. I heard a chuckle. "Well, well, the little '@#*!' showed up, eh?"

I was ushered in. His secretary followed his command and got someone on the phone in Sun Valley. The conversation I heard was:

"Hi Pat, I have a young skier wants to come out and train with our new Swedish coach, so send a train ticket to Sun Valley, and find him a job and a place to live."

My benefactor turned out to be Al Lindley, a wealthy attorney and super sportsman, high in the ranks of the U.S. Ski Association. The man he called was Pat Rogers, manager of Sun Valley.

I trained with the new coach, Lief Odmark and went to the trials out East where I was able to make the team.

Yup, Lutsen was important to me some years back and I was certainly lucky to be there that day."

George Hovland would have a stellar skiing career. Among his numerous accomplishments are competing in the 1952

Winter Olympics in Oslo and being the first non-European to complete the Swedish 90-kilometer Vasaloppet.

After Lutsen's first ski season, separate engines are installed to power the towropes on Chickadee and Koo Koo. These early engines are high maintenance. Although the engines are six-volt, on extremely cold days two six-volt batteries are needed to produce sufficient power to start the engines. Often, even that is not enough and workers have to burn oil in a baking pan to warm the engines before they will fire up.

The sparkle of the early days is reflected in a story about George Jr.'s uncle Oscar, who serves as ticket-seller when the ski hill opens. One day, a young lady asks why she should buy a ticket to ride the lift up the ski hill when she can as easily walk. Oscar replies that he will give her a deal – for $3, he will let her walk up the hill all day.

Another memorable character working at the ski area in the early days is Errol "Unk" Worthing, a night watchman who carries a World War I German Luger pistol. If Unk suspects *"...someone is up to no good..."* he fires a couple of rounds into the air, just to let any potential troublemakers know he is there – and ready.

In spring, after the snow melts, Unk collects coins that have been dropped along the ski runs.

Remarkably, with all the work and commotion related to the ski area, the main resort reopens in February 1949, albeit on a limited scale. Rooms are available in the only building on top of the hill to survive both fires of the previous year. The dining room also reopens with meals served while construction takes place behind a large canvas draped along one side of the room. The ongoing work has no effect on the food or service, which diners report to be as good as ever. There is no grand opening yet (that will not happen until the building is completed).

An interesting aside appears in the News Herald of March 3:

"Mr. Nelson and son George got together for some skiing in one of the Northern Michigan ski areas."

Presumably, the pair was trying to learn something to improve their ski area.

Due to unfavorable weather, the ski resort does not open its second season until New Year's Day, 1950. Even then, it is a wet and mild day with sticky snow, hardly ideal for skiing.

That same month, George Jr. wins one of only four awards from the Canadian Amateur Ski Association, achieving top honors for best all round skill. To get his award, George Jr. has to pass rigid tests in first aid, all around skiing skill, theory and instruction in skiing. George Sr. comes close to winning an award, losing out in only one area. Both men return to Lutsen, eager to instill some of their acquired knowledge in local students during the ski season.

As the season progresses, winter business at the ski area exceeds expectations. There is also a change in when skiers are coming to the resort. At first, all business is on weekends by reservation but as the season wears on, more people begin coming during the week without reservations. This is encouraging, indicating that skiers are becoming more familiar with the setup and that weekday business will continue to pick up.

Such is not the case for the Greyhound Bus Company, which removes Lutsen as a stop along its North Shore route.

Unfortunately, other travelers are hitching rides to Lake Superior. The invasion of lamprey throughout the coming decade will deal a tremendous blow to the commercial fishing industry, reducing the number of commercial fisherman from several hundred to just a few.

At about the same time, George Jr. graduates from Michigan State University with a degree in Hotel Administration. Returning to Lutsen, he resumes his wooing of Patti and the couple marries at the Grand Marais Lutheran church in November 1950. For their honeymoon, they embark on a cross-country tour, with George Jr. admiring the best ski spots along the way. When they return to Lutsen, Patti becomes more involved in the daily operation of the resort, taking charge of the ski school and gift shops, and improving the food service by offering more selections, such as lamb, frog legs, salad bar and smorgasbord.

The following year sees a major addition to the Lutsen community when the Mount Olivet Cathedral of the Pines Camp is dedicated in August, with Governor Youngdahl delivering the dedicatory address. The camp is located on Caribou Lake on the site of the old Northern Lights resort, once owned by the Lyght family but sold in 1948.

🐾 CHAPTER 28 🐾

REDUCED TO ASHES

Unbelievably, disaster strikes Lutsen again in December, 1951. This time, an electrical fire in the laundry room below the dining room results in the resort lodge being a complete loss.

The News Herald reports the damage in its edition of December 6:

"LUTSEN RESORT FIRE

Lutsen Resort Again Lost by Fire: Loss is $300,000.
People weep as flames level still incomplete structure.

Crowds of tearful spectators watched helplessly as the new Lutsen Resort was reduced to ashes in a very short space of time Tuesday morning, the second time the resort has burned in 3 years. The $300,000 building of Swedish design, embodying much hand hewn carving, was still unfinished but had been used for the past 3 seasons. The resort was owned by the Lutsen Resorts, Inc. In this company are the George Nelson Sr. and Jr. families.

Word flashed about the county shortly after seven o'clock Tuesday morning that the 30-room structure was on fire and people just could not believe their ears. Many of them drove to the fire to see for themselves and by the time they arrived, there was nothing but an inferno of flames licking at the bases of the still standing chimneys. Now and then muffled sounds of explosions were heard.

George Nelson Sr. said the fire, of unknown origin, started in the laundry in the basement under the dining room. He had been there shortly before to start a motor that had stopped, which should have supplied water pressure to the rooms. After leaving, he went up to the third floor where the Nelsons had their living quarters and not long after heard cries of "Fire!"

A group of about 40 Bell Telephone executives from all over the Midwest, who were staying at the resort for a week, was having breakfast and noticed smoke seeping out through the walls. They rushed to their rooms to get their belongings and

*call out warnings. Mrs. Nelson meantime had been in the
kitchen where the chef was making pancakes. She noticed more
smoke than usual but thought it was from pancake frying. When
she entered the dining room, guests were already rushing to their
rooms. From that time on, there was little time to save anything.
Some personal belongings were lost by staff as well as the
Nelsons. It is believed that the guests were able to save what they
had with them.*

*Instead of the usual wise cracking that is often heard at fires,
there were sounds of sobbing and tears in men's eyes.
Everywhere they were of the same opinion: "This was a great
loss to the whole North Shore." All hearts went out to the
Nelsons who were, in Mr. Nelson's own words, "Just beginning
to breathe again."*

*Just what plans for the future may be depends on many
things, Mr. Nelson said. "If I want to stay here, I suppose I will
have to rebuild." But there are problems of building priorities,
insurance, sky-high building costs, and the like that loom up at
once. If these can be overcome, there is some likelihood the
Nelsons will rebuild. Added to the great loss is the loss of
potential business on a year round basis. Many reservations were
already in for skiing season that was likely to start any day. Next
summer's business would also be lost.*

*The original Lutsen resort burned to the ground in the early
hours of October 18, 1948. That too was a complete loss but it
was in that fire that many relics from the early history of the
North Shore were also burned. The loss then was estimated at
$200,000. That same year the Nelsons lost one of their large
dormitories so this is their third loss by fire in a span of less than
four years."*

It is rumored that faulty wiring is the cause of this latest blaze
but after a careful review, the deputy fire marshal states that the
wiring met building codes. He speculates that there may have
been a mechanical failure in the main entry box. Some,
however, believe the cause to be a power surge that occurs when
the local power plant switches from nighttime to daytime
operation. Nevertheless, no definite explanation for the fire is
ever made public.

Almost three months pass before a rebuilding decision is announced on February 21, 1952 by George Sr., with work expected to commence in 30 days. The structure will follow the same plans as the previous building, with a Swedish architectural style, hewn posts, hand carved doors and a large, stone fireplace. It is hoped to have the main dining room in operation by July and the rest of the business up and running the following winter.

The footings, hallway, entryway, steps and fireplace rock from the ruined structure are salvaged and used in the new building. Unfortunately, the virgin white Pine from Lake Agnes is lost and replaced with wood from a Gunflint Trail lumberyard.

Architect Edwin Lundie oversees the rebuilding. Years later, he would recall his excitement in finding that:

"All of the elements for an indigenous architecture were present. The bold scale of the rugged coast, the background of the forest, the intriguing beauty of the building sites, and then the great sweep of Lake Superior provided reason for a particular concept. Present were the materials, the lumber and timber from surrounding forests, the stone from the hills and present also were the skills of the artisan and craftsman to be explored, encouraged and exploited."

Inspired by the historical styles of Normandy and Scandinavia and knowledgeable about colonial American architecture, Lundie sets about building his vision. Features reflect the scale of the surrounding geography, beginning with the resort road sign, held out to Highway 61 by a large obelisk post. On the other side of the property, the lodge's broad façade reflects the lake it faces. Approaching the main lodge, the entry porch extends a welcome and invites visitors inside. Built from native firs, the lodge continues to emphasize grandeur with massive corner posts and the lobby's great fireplace, flanked by large windows and spanned by oversized, carved beams.

Offsetting this size are details hand-carved by skilled local craftspeople. Examples of their work can be seen in how spindles attach to the banister and treads to stringers on the main staircase. Apart from visual beauty, these details offer a sense of intimacy.

The original gas station is the only building to survive the fire. New structures added as part of the rebuilding include the red road sign, fence posts, a swimming pool and covered bridges across the Poplar River. Many smaller cabins are planned but are never built.

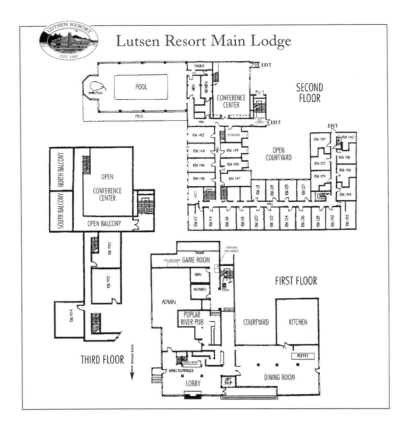

Floor plan of the rebuilt Lutsen Resort

The fire causes the denizens of Lutsen to finally recognize that it might be prudent to invest in the purchase of a fire truck for their small, volunteer fire department. A truck is finally purchased from the Air Force, which used the vehicle as a runway fire unit at the old Wold-Chamberlain Airfield in

Minneapolis. After the purchase, the fire department makes it known that donations and paid-in pledges are not enough to cover the entire cost and a bank loan has been taken out. People who want fire protection, along with those who have not paid their pledges, are reminded to *"...see the committee."* This is the first time a Cook County community outside Grand Marais has secured such sophisticated fire equipment but that is not surprising, given the mutual commitment between the Lutsen community and its firefighters.

The Lutsen Volunteer Fire Department is the first locally financed organization of its type in the county. It receives no federal, state or county aid and has no local levy to depend on. The volunteers receive no pay for their efforts. When they leave their jobs to fight a fire, it is money out of their pockets. They also pay their own expenses when travelling in search of new equipment or to fight fires in other communities. When something is needed, the department solicits help from the local community and people give according to their ability. By these means, over the next few years the department is able to acquire equipment such as a backup water truck, a siren for the fire hall and top quality boots, coats, hats, oxygen packs and other equipment, long before most communities have such necessities. Over the years, the Lutsen Volunteer Fire Department is recognized as a model for other small communities.

Lutsen Fire Department volunteers

❧ CHAPTER 29 ❧

BOOM AND BUST

The ski area remains busy, with two rope tows being added. The town is also growing. Early in 1953, the Lutheran parish separates from Grand Marais and combines with Tofte. In February, an airport is proposed.

Technology advances and on May 16, 1955, dial telephone service arrives in Lutsen. The phone company promises there will be no more than eight parties on each line and a new ringing arrangement will allow each party to hear only one ring in addition to their own.

In 1955, Lutsen's most famous citizen is born. Cindy Nelson will win an Olympic bronze medal at the 1976 Olympic Games at Innsbruck, Austria and World Championship Silver medals in 1980 and 1982. No one imagined this when Cindy began to ski at age two. One early outing is not indicative of her later skills but does hint at her courage. Skiing down a small hill, she cannot stop and skis into a parking lot and slides under a car. Everyone is frightened but Cindy is uninjured. *"I got my suit dirty,"* she says guiltily.

In early December of that year, at 4 p.m. on a Friday, technology improves again. A switch is turned on and the Minnesota Power and Light Company transmission system begins providing electricity to Lutsen. The old, obsolete power plant falls idle, soon to be used as an office and warehouse.

Other sources of enlightenment are also under consideration for modernization. A new church is planned and the Lutheran Brotherhood is approached for a loan. The Brotherhood is astonished to find that only a $10,000 mortgage is needed, since most funds will come from the local community. This is the smallest mortgage the Brotherhood has ever approved. The old church building, originally hauled from Grand Marais, is moved again, this time, a short distance west. It serves the community for a number of years as a recreation center and later as the Birch Grove school gymnasium, before being torn down.

Ground for the new Lutsen Evangelical Lutheran church is broken at 3 p.m. on Sunday, May 19, 1957. Plans are for the construction to be by volunteer labor, including 12 students from St. Olaf College in Northfield. The number of students is unrelated to the disciples mentioned in scripture. Work is to be completed during the summer.

The vision for the new church is that it will be:
"Standing on an elevated triangular plot surrounded by a retaining wall of native rock, the new building is to be 30 by 68 feet. An adjoining narthex will measure eight by 16 feet. The building will have a contemporary design with a knotty pine interior. The auditorium will have a simple arrangement with a choir loft and organ at the rear. The altar, pulpit, and baptismal font will be backed by a wall of glass overlooking Lake Superior.

Decorative color will add life to the pine and stone materials, with a backing of greens behind the altar and Swedish red exterior walls. Natural lighting from three sides will provide a cheerful atmosphere. A freestanding bell tower will occupy the south angle of the retaining wall."

*Architect's drawing of the new
Lutsen Evangelical Lutheran church*

The finished church

Construction, however, takes longer than expected and the church will not hold its first services until June 7, 1959, with dedication on July 11.

The resort is also undergoing construction. A 20 by 45 feet heated swimming pool with depths ranging from two to eight feet, is built north of the lodge. A large deck area surrounds the pool, which is lighted for night swimming. Because of state law, users are required to take showers but since normally only guests have access to showers, daily visitor rates are offered to the public, allowing the use of showers with no fee for use of the pool.

The September grand opening of the pool is quite an event. George Sr. unexpectedly initiates the pool before assembled guests when he is presented with a hand-knit swimsuit – served to him on a silver serving tray - and told to jump in even though the pool has not yet been heated. Staged by resort employees, the event program features demonstrations on life-saving and water safety, diving, a synchronized swim ballet performed to the tune of "While We're Young", and "*A day in the life of a waitress, demonstrated by swimming and diving."* It is said that the pool, with its underwater lighting, looks beautiful at night. Its look, however, will change.

Just over a year later, an air-supported, plastic bubble is erected over the pool to enable swimming throughout winter. It is the first such bubble set over a swimming pool anywhere. The Schjeldome, as it is called, covers a 73 by 36 feet area, embracing the pool and deck area. Standing 18 feet tall, the dome connects to the main lodge by a plastic breezeway that shields swimmers from winter air as they go to and from the pool.

The bubble is supported entirely by forced air. When a door opens, some air escapes but is automatically replaced by pumps. Both water and air are heated and the bubble is transparent so the wintery landscape outside can be seen from inside. Made from a tough Mylar material, the dome can withstand gales of up to 100 miles per hour.

After two years, however, the bubble is removed. A spate of vandalism at the resort creates a risk that the Mylar will be slashed and the structure will collapse around anyone inside.

The Lutsen Resort Swimming Pool Bubble

Not content with the swimming pool, the Nelsons make a fateful decision, announced in the September 19 edition of the News Herald:

"Lutsen Resort is building a nine-hole golf course. It is situated on the hill near the Cliff House and will have grass greens. Because of the limited space, fairways will be relatively short, wood drivers will not be used. The course, however, will fill a long-felt need in giving guests another activity and golf is always popular."

When the golf course opens in May, it is touted as *"... an irons course which will test anyone's ability."*

While facilities such as the pool and golf course provide opportunities to enjoy recreational and sporting activities, the resort also provides cultural opportunities not otherwise available to locals. For example, on July 11, 1958, the resort hosts *"The best exhibition of photographic art ever shown in Minnesota."* This is according to Clarence Stearns, past President of the Photographers' Association of America, who continues, *"This exhibit will display some of the finest modern portraiture as well as community and pictorial photography."*

Skiing, however, is the most popular pastime on the North Shore and major improvements are made to accommodations and facilities. Most important among these is the installation of a Poma ski lift. The lift consists of 66 hanger discs, on which skiers sit while holding a center pole as they are pulled up the hill. This is less tiring than being pulled uphill by the hands.

Poma ski lift

The lift is 2,640 feet long and pulls riders up the hill at a fast rate. However, the Poma cannot be used for summer sightseeing, as riders must stand on skis as they ascend.

In addition, a new ski run is cut, the chalet is expanded and a new bridge is built across the highway.

To prepare for the expected increase in business, the Cliff House hilltop dormitory near the lake is winterized, doubling the seasonal capacity of the resort to 250. More importantly, six Tofte, Lutsen and Grand Marais businesses enter into a cooperative advertising arrangement. This is done to assure wary skiers who might feel accommodations are lacking if only one resort is listed. Finally, there is a new offer under which a reduced rate activities card can be used for swimming, golfing and skiing.

In March of 1960, an old project resurfaces when the Cook County Board receives a letter from Federal engineering authorities, asking about the need for a refuge harbor at Lutsen. It is noted that such a project requires:

- About $94,000 in local funds (along with $640,000 in federal funding).

- Local provision and maintenance of a public wharf for the accommodation of transient vessels.

- A local public body to regulate use and development of the harbor.

- Provision of all lands and rights of way for construction and spoilage disposal.

- Holding and saving the U.S. free from damages related to the project.

Cook County replies that there is currently no need or financial ability to pay for such a project, nor is there a local organization capable of providing cooperation. Accordingly, on April 29, the project is inactivated by the Chief of Engineers.

In December, George Jr. makes his considerable instruction skills available by opening a ski school at the Lutsen ski area. The area's reputation is by now such that in April of 1961, it is announced that the 1962 Regional Alpine Boys' and Girls' Championship will be held there.

In July 1961, the final addition is made to the Lundie-designed resort when a new rustic sign, made from white pine, is hung along Highway 61. Designed in a Swedish motif to harmonize with the character of the main lodge, the sign has hand-carved, gilded lettering. George Sr. has spent five years hunting for a white pine large enough to meet his requirements.

Original roadside sign

New roadside sign

The following year, Minnesota's moose population numbers only about 3,000. Even worse is the Lake Superior fish population. According to Carl Nelson, lamprey infestation has made it hard to find enough fish to eat, never mind to sell. In an interview, he offers a chilling assessment: *"No-one can live by fishing now. The lamprey will only die off when there are no fish left."*

Carl is prophetic. In 1879 there were 37 men fishing commercially on the lake. By 1917, about 280 men had commercial fishing licenses. In the peak years during World War II, when demand was heavy, there were as many as 450 fishermen or one for every 600 yards of shoreline from Duluth to Grand Portage. A few years after Carl's pessimistic forecast, only about 10 commercial fishermen remain along the shore.

No one knows it at the time but February 21, 1963 provides a glimpse into what makes a champion. Cindy Nelson, age nine, finishes third in a local ski race. What is special about the result is that Cindy finishes the race on only one ski. When her other ski comes off, Cindy knows she cannot take time to put it back on and so comes through on one ski. At such a young age, Cindy already displays an ability to assess and control situations, using determination, courage and skill.

Since Lutsen is no longer a town, it has no use for a Town Hall and the building becomes a school until its students are sent to the new Tofte School. After that, the Town Hall falls into disuse until early 1964 when George Jr. purchases the building to use for storage.

Remember that an airport was proposed for Lutsen back in 1953. No one had taken the proposal seriously but on July 27, 1964, an airport is dedicated at the Cathedral of the Pines site.

🐾 CHAPTER 30 🐾

THE TROUBLE WITH BEARS

During the summer of 1964, bears feature prominently around the Lutsen area. There are frequent sightings of the animals at the Lutsen dumpsite. Tourists and locals gather to watch up to 30 bears at a time at the Caribou Trail site. Observers particularly enjoy the antics of cubs and find brown bears more appealing because of their thicker fur. The bear activity is reported as far away as Rochester, Minnesota. Given its sudden fame as a tourist attraction, the site is cleaned up, trees are planted, walks laid and signs hung. Such are the improvements that Willard Nelson observes dryly, *"You have to put on a white shirt now to go to the new-look Lutsen dump."* Obviously, such etiquette does not apply to bears.

A second significant incident concerning a bear occurs at the resort in mid-September. At 3 a.m. George Sr.'s wife, Inga, awakens to noises on the roof. George Sr. goes downstairs to investigate. He finds the night watchman in a dither. The man has just come from the kitchen where he encountered a bear that has torn an extractor fan out of the wall and entered the kitchen through the vent. On impulse, the man, who has a hook instead of a hand on one arm, grabbed a broom and awkwardly shooed the bear out the same hole by which he had entered.

Meanwhile, from her bed, Inga can still hear the noises. Getting up, she looks out her third floor window and is horrified to see the bear on the second-story roof, looking in at her. Her screams fetch George Sr. rather quickly. Grabbing a gun, he fires at the bear but misses. Seeing that the odds are now against him, the bear jumps onto the swimming pool roof below. The corrugated plastic roof affords no traction and the bear slides all the way to the ground, and then scampers into the darkness, leaving George and Inga laughing at his unbecoming escape.

The famous evangelist Dr. Billy Graham misses this episode when he shows up at the resort a few days later. He may have been glad to avoid the commotion, since the News Herald reports that he is:

"...there just to relax, he and his companion golfed on the resort course, swam in the pool and seemed to enjoy the autumn foliage."

Back in the business world, the ski area is about to undergo rapid and large expansion over the next two years. A large part of the expansion will center on Mystery Mountain, which was named in a curious way: The U.S. Forest Service owns land on two sides of the ski area. George Jr. wants to add a ski run on a mountain he believes to be on Nelson property. Wanting to be sure, he hires a surveyor to confirm who owns the mountain. The surveyor reports that the peak is indeed on Nelson land and asks for the mountain's name. *"It's a mystery to me,"* George Jr. replies. *"That's good enough,"* responds the surveyor and so Mystery Mountain is christened.

The ski area expansion includes an additional Poma lift and a double chair lift that can carry 1,200 skiers an hour up 2,450 feet along a 502 ft vertical drop hill. New ski slopes, up to one and a half miles long and a new ski chalet are also built.

New Chalet in the Making

Here is an architect's drawing of the new Lutsen chalet.

New snowmaking and grooming equipment on all major
slopes will assure excellent skiing conditions whether it snows or
not. Water for snowmaking will be forced up from the Poplar
River through special aluminum pipes. Forced air will be
pushed through another set of pipes and mixed with the water to
make snow. The improvements will create a need for more
lodging.

For George Jr., the work will also create a need for medical
attention. In September, he is working on a Poma lift tower
when the ladder he is standing on breaks and he falls 25 feet,
landing in mud and having his head narrowly miss the concrete
base of the tower. Another worker witnesses the accident and
straps him on a bombardier, which is the only vehicle at hand.
Taken to a car, he is rushed to the local hospital. Although he is
unconscious for a few hours, a preliminary examination shows
only cuts, bruises and two broken ribs. The relatively slight
injuries are due to the muddy landing that cushioned the fall.
Luckily, the wooden frame around the concrete base had been
removed or his head would have hit that, with Humpty-
Dumptyish results. He spends several days in the hospital for
observation.

Along with the ski area expansion, the Lutsen resort sees two
other notable additions during 1965. First, the resort is granted a
liquor license that also covers the ski area. This is allowed
because of a pipe that runs from the resort to a spot under the
Highway 61 Poplar River Bridge, making the main resort and
the ski area *"contiguous facilities."* Second, a WATS telephone
line with an 800 number is installed.

The town of Lutsen suffers an economic blow when the
Hansen's store, opened in 1928 and owned by the same family
ever since, goes out of business.

December sees the start of an early ski season and the impact
of the ongoing expansion is already apparent, with record
crowds showing up during the holiday weeks. On some days,
there are around 600 paid admissions and season ticket holders
using the facilities. Increased parking needs and waiting times at
the lifts threaten to become major problems if the crowds
continue to grow. Accommodations in Tofte, Lutsen and Grand

Marais are filled to capacity. While the early snow makes for great skiing, it slows work on the new chalet. However, although full chalet service is not available, the ground floor area is far enough along to take care of skiers. The new Mystery Mountain development is an immense improvement to the area and skiers eagerly anticipate the new mile and a half ski run, served by a 4,500 feet Poma lift. This will be the longest intermediate run in Minnesota, Wisconsin or Michigan.

In the spring of 1966, the ski resort hosts the Midwest Divisional Junior Ski Meet, a major event, with 150 skiers from Minnesota, Wisconsin, Michigan, Illinois, Ohio and North Dakota. The event introduces a major innovation to the area by using electronic timing. This eliminates human error in timings as each skier breaks an electrical current at the start and finish of the race, with skiers' times recorded electronically. Previously, a starter at the top of the hill spoke into a phone with a countdown, which was synchronized by a chief timer at the finish line. At the word "*Go!*", three stopwatches were set in motion and when the skier crossed the finish line, timers stopped their watches. There were often variances in timing of as much as several tenths of a second, due to distances, reflexes of timers and other reasons. The chief timer then decided on an average for the final time. With electronic timing, variances are eliminated. Prudently, however, standby manual timers are at the ready, in case something goes wrong.

❧ CHAPTER 31 ❧

HOT-DOGGING

At the beginning of 1968, the Duluth News Tribune Outlook newspaper reveals an idea that will revolutionize the North Shore housing and tourism industries. The plan is to build a new townhouse development at Lutsen, an idea born to solve two problems: The first is the need for additional housing at Lutsen during the peak winter and summer seasons. The second problem has challenged recreation-minded families for years: How to own a nice vacation home at a reasonable cost? One answer to both problems seems to be condominium-type vacation homes. Highly successful in many parts of the country, the concept allows a family's vacation home to be rented when not in use.

In the fall of 1968, the idea is implemented as construction begins on the first phase of the Lutsen Sea Villas. Eventually, there will be 52 villas. A villa owner can recover a large portion of the purchase cost through rental when the owner is not using the property. Among the benefits to all parties are that the buyer acquires property with help from others, the renter gets a place to stay at a reasonable cost and the area has more accommodations available. The entire community also gains increased winter and summer business.

The villas are a huge success and there is soon a list of about 300 people interested in owning one, although only about 10% are expected to close the purchase. However, the building of new units is halted because the resort does not want to dominate competition with its neighbors.

As if he is not busy enough with condominium development, George Jr. oversees completion of the convention hall and recreation room that connect the main lodge to the swimming pool.

However, not every new Lutsen business venture is a success. One example of a good idea not well implemented, is the Par 3 golf course the resort owners build on the south side of Highway 61. It is a noble effort that recognizes the role golf can play in attracting visitors to the area. Because of its beautifully manicured grass, soil from the Lutsen church is used for the course greens. Alas, not even the thought of playing on holy ground is sufficient to entice the numbers of golfers expected. Usually planners on an impressive scale, this time the Nelsons' product is not grand enough, comprising only nine holes. Golfers making the trip to Lutsen want 18 holes and when they find only a short course is available, one third of reservations are cancelled. Usually, the cancellations come too late for the resort to take replacement bookings.

Skiing, however, is all the rage and the 1970s begin with business at the ski area hitting an all-time high. Excellent snow conditions, favorable weather and increased interest in the sport contribute to the increase but the availability of more housing in the area, bolstered by the new villas, is mostly responsible for the large influx of ski enthusiasts. Fortunately, thinking ahead as usual, George Jr. has installed two new lifts and has rebuilt an existing one, thus alleviating the issue of waiting for lifts.

Despite the booming business and recent expansion, George Jr. believes the potential for winter business has barely been scratched and further expansion of the ski area is needed to realize this potential. Given the number of expansions so far, it may seem that adding to and improving the ski area should by now be a simple matter. It is not. Funding is often a problem, despite general acknowledgement that skiing has a strong impact on North Shore business and expansion would strengthen the area's economy. Generalities, however, are not as effective as showing a direct impact on bottom lines and George Jr. invests a huge amount of time making the case for expansion. This expansion proposal provides insight into the process and illustrates how important skiing has become to the North Shore economy.

In April 1970, a public meeting is held at the Grand Marais courthouse to discuss the proposed expansion. Everyone agrees the expansion should be pursued and a committee is formed to get local participation to obtain financing for the expansion program. Then things slow down.

Because of the lack of progress, George Jr. is much more specific about the benefits of expansion at a second meeting in February 1971. He points out that his winter business, coupled with the Sea Villa project have been a direct benefit to the whole county through increased income from taxation and from filling rooming accommodations during peak periods. The Sea Villa project alone, he says, has generated about $10,000 in taxes to the county.

George Jr. also points out that he will be changing his advertising from television commercials to an expanded reservations system that will use two WATS telephone lines. The resort has been using a single WATS line for reservations within Minnesota for four years and is the first resort in the state to have done so. The new reservations system will cover a 10-state area. This is important for other resort owners because when the Lutsen desk clerk answers a call, information is taken from the prospective guest as to desires and needs. A reservation is then placed with an appropriate accommodation, even if it is a Lutsen competitor. These reservations are at no charge to the competitor, even though the cost of each placement is approximately $5. These costs cover leasing the telephone line and expenses for advertising and promotional publicity such as information packets, mailings and stickers.

It takes a while but George Jr. finally succeeds in convincing local stakeholders that what is good for Lutsen is good for them and they throw their support behind the expansion plans. Consequently, in August 1972, the ski area adds two new high capacity, double chair lifts to its popular slopes. Together they increase uphill capacity more than 50%.

Business remains good until Lutsen is struck by the worldwide energy crisis in 1973. Faced with the possibility of reduced patronage of his ski area due to the closing of gas stations, George Jr. realizes that energy saving plans being considered by Twin Cities' schools, could benefit North Shore businesses. Three-day weekends and closing schools for up to one month during the coldest part of winter will provide extra time for recreation. Therefore, George Jr. develops a plan to transport skiers from the Twin Cities on chartered buses.

The Medicine Lake Bus Company is contracted to furnish buses, with service to begin in mid-December. A Twin Cities office handles reservations for accommodations in Cook County. Two sales representatives solicit business and a newspaper advertising campaign is launched to promote the service. Buses leave the Twin Cities each Friday, stopping at motels between Schroeder and Grand Marais. Shuttle service and meals for the skiers are developed with the businesses that furnish accommodations. Most skiers stay in Grand Marais and are shuttled back and forth to the slopes. Return trips to Minneapolis and St. Paul are on Sundays.

The battle to maintain and promote the ski business includes several other initiatives. One is a "hot-dogging" or aerial stunt skiing competition to be held at Lutsen. In conjunction with this event, former world champion Billy Kidd and other national hot-doggers will film a TV series – *The American Ski Scene* – at Lutsen throughout the winter. Local skiing enthusiasts will therefore see, and it is hoped, be inspired by some of the top performing skiers in the nation.

Another initiative is the introduction of a ski ministry. These half-hour worship experiences feature an abbreviated, informal style with guitars and music in the "modern mode."

Cross-country skiing opportunities are also increased, with trails being re-graded and expanded. By the end of 1975, the ski area has 16 miles of marked trails, with ski rentals and instruction available. There is also a cabin available for overnight trips.

The following January, "Airborn (sic) Eddie Ferguson," the world champion of freestyle hot-dog skiing, appears at Lutsen to participate in a demonstration and hot-dog contest. The teaching of freestyle skiing is included in the weekend activities.

Despite the battle to maintain business, George Jr. continues to show consideration for his competitors when he donates a towrope to the Sawtooth Mountain Ski Hill outside Grand Marais.

The huge success of the ski area creates an issue related to the Ski Hill Road. The two-mile road is the sole automobile access to the ski area. In 1975, George Jr. begins to push for the narrow dirt road to be improved, since it has several safety hazards, including a steep gradient and several large curves. George Jr. thinks the road should be paved, widened and have the dangerous curves removed. He is flabbergasted to learn that in 1973 the State of Minnesota reviewed the volume of traffic using the road and counted a daily average of 30 vehicles, not enough to give the road priority for upgrading. Unconvinced, George Jr. performs his own count and finds the daily average to be over 2,000 trips! Nonetheless, it is 1981 before the road is finally improved.

Meanwhile, a strong competitor to the ski area has emerged and is having a large impact on the Lutsen Ski Area's business. Duluth's Spirit Mountain has brought growth at Lutsen to a standstill for two years and has especially slowed early season skiing. Some had thought the Duluth facility would help Lutsen by sparking greater interest in skiing but this is not the case. It is difficult for Lutsen to compete with Spirit Mountain. For one thing, Lutsen has to find its own financing, whereas Spirit Mountain has access to grant money that does not have to be repaid. The Duluth resort also hurts midweek skiing at Lutsen. There used to be ski buses going to Lutsen from Duluth but those people now stay in Duluth to ski.

Trying to keep up with the demands of the main resort and the ski area while dealing with the Duluth competition, is too much for one person and George Jr. is feeling the strain. Patti is not a manager but she can see problems developing. She tells her husband he needs to hire some help. George Jr. takes her advice and on June 10, 1976, Phil Peterson is named President of the Lutsen Ski Association

Phil launches an all-out offensive on several fronts to bolster the Lutsen ski and tourist industry. About 80 ski club presidents from cities throughout the Midwest are invited for an all-expenses-paid weekend at Lutsen. The presidents are lodged at the Sea Villas and treated to a variety of functions, dances, races, free ski lessons, cross-country tours, and other entertainment. Local motel and hotel operators are invited to help the presidents line up accommodations for future ski trips for their clubs. That same weekend, about 75 salespeople from various Minnesota ski shops are also treated to a weekend of skiing.

Improvements are made to the ski area with the addition of more snow making equipment and improved existing snow machines. Grooming equipment is also upgraded.

Lutsen is selected as one of five major ski areas in the U.S. and the only one in the Midwest to offer family challenge racing. Lutsen offers this program in three categories: mother/son, father/daughter, and best family. The top family receives an expense-paid trip to Utah to spend three days at the U.S. Olympic training center skiing with the Olympic team.

Lutsen also becomes the only ski area in the Midwest to offer free skiing to youngsters under 10 and to offer special lessons for children. Adult instruction is not neglected. The ski school is expanded to include 12 highly trained instructors for downhill, cross-country and freestyle skiing. To stoke interest in cross-country skiing, new trails are added. Unique half day and full day cross-country tours include instruction, with bonfires and lunches along the trail.

More improvements are planned and George Jr. turns to the Small Business Administration for help. It is more than eager to assist a "depressed area." This worries George Jr., since he does not think of Lutsen as depressed. He does not realize that all of Cook County is considered depressed.

In July 1977, funding is in place for $700,000 worth of summer and winter recreation. The star attraction will be a summer activity, practiced on the slopes of the winter ski area. Phil and George Jr. have traveled across the country for six months to study the attraction, which originated in Europe and was only introduced to the U.S. in 1976. Longer than six football fields, there are only six such attractions throughout the country and Lutsen's will be the only one in the Midwest. Capable of travelling up to 15 miles per hour or being slowed to a crawl, the attraction is advertised as allowing summer vacationers of all ages to safely experience some of the thrills of skiing.

The Lutsen alpine slide opens on August 12, 1977. The traditional ribbon-cutting ceremony is performed by Minnesota

Lt. Gov. Alec Olson who rides down the 2,200 feet slide and through the ribbon. Costing $400,000 the slide is capable of carrying up to 200,000 riders during the summer. It will provide 30 summer jobs, a notable impact in a depressed area. The ski chalet will now have a summer use as a restaurant for sliders.

George Nelson Jr. (left) and Minnesota Lt. Gov. Alec Olson inaugurate the alpine slide at Lutsen

After the launching of the alpine slide, attention turns to the skiing improvements. While funding has been secured, there is a potential snag. George Jr. cannot get the funds until September and he worries that the ground will need to be worked before fall frost turns the land to mud. However, his luck holds and work is able to proceed. Snow making capacity increases with the purchase of two more snow making machines, six snow making guns and water pumps with new piping to draw water from the Poplar River. However, this creates a problem. Snowmaking systems are designed to use water at a temperature of 48 degrees. Water from the Poplar is about 33 degrees and when mixed with air to make snow, freezes the snowmaking guns. This problem is solved by using boilers to heat the water to 48 degrees.

One advantage of snowmaking equipment is the availability of water to fight fires on the ski slopes. This is demonstrated in

February of 1978 when a garage catches fire at the ski area. Built in 1947, the structure was the original ski chalet. Firemen are able to use water from the snowmaking machines to prevent damage to a nearby chair lift.

By the time the improvements are completed, Lutsen has expanded its cross-country ski trails to cover over 20 miles. More importantly, by extending the skiing season one month, the improvements finally make Lutsen a year-round tourist destination.

🐾 CHAPTER 32 🐾

A LION, AN ARAB, AND SCAVENGERS

S ome unusual events are taking place around Lutsen in the early part of 1978.

On March 9, the News Herald reports:

"Lutsen Lion Is No More

Slugs from three high-powered rifles killed Simba the lion, owned by Dick Maw of Lutsen, on Monday 2/27. Simba, who lived with the Maws for over six years, escaped from his cage by pushing through a portion of the fencing. Mrs. Maw called neighbors and the Cook County Sheriff, requesting that the animal be killed. Three law enforcement officers went to the Maw's residence and fired their rifles simultaneously, dropping Simba next to the dog kennels. He never suffered.

Maw said the lion had only attempted to escape once before, when a pack of wolves came off the lake and milled about his pen. The lion nearly tore down the wood fence to get at the wolves."

Maw had purchased Simba from the Minneapolis Zoo several years earlier, thinking the black-maned cub would make a fine tourist attraction. He hires Jim W. Anderson, a local hunter, to shoot and butcher old cattle and horses to feed the lion. After the lion's death, Maw asks Anderson to skin the big cat. Anderson agrees to do so for $50 and describes the task:

"She had front feet the size of two-dollar pizza and just as tough. The tail was stiffer than the main line on a new skidder. The hide yielded a seventy-five pound fur coat. I used the carcass for fox and coyote trapping bait but no wild animal would go near it. Even the ravens were skeptical for months, until they got hungry enough to pick the bones clean."

Simba, the Lutsen lion

At the end of the month, the newspaper carries another intriguing article:

"Famous Sheik Flaps Down Koo-Koo

A famous Lebanon sheik, Sheik Saleim Abdul Haddad, faced Cindy Nelson on the Lutsen slopes during the Special Celebrity-Am race held there Saturday as part of Lutsen's Easter Spring Fest. About 850 spectators were on hand to see the event. There is still some question as to who won the event. Because of his full Arab regalia and flowing robes, it was difficult to determine exactly when the sheik's body crossed the finish line. Cindy, who was home for about 4 days last week, before leaving for five more races with the US ski team, spent the afternoon racing other skiers on Lutsen's KooKoo. She and the sheik helped raise over $600, which will be donated to the US ski team. The sheik is a worldwide celebrity, especially after some questions were raised regarding his true national origins. He first appeared at the Winter Park Pro-Am race in Colorado and his flowing robes were pictured in over 450 major newspapers in America. Six large European dailies called the UPI for special color photos, which they ran on their front pages. Specially opened for the weekend was the alpine slide at Lutsen."

Ski clothing has always been pretty colorful, but Sheikh Saleim Abdul Haddad outdid everyone on the slopes of Lutsen last weekend. He and Cindy Nelson compared racing strategies after their run down Koo-Koo Saturday afternoon. Later, the Sheik tried the Alpine Slide.

It can now be revealed that the mysterious sheik was a member of a family that owned a Persian carpet store in Duluth.

Meanwhile, as he has done for many years, Clarence Larson, a maintenance worker at the resort, continues to drive the resort garbage truck, a 1937 Buick LTD that has been sawn off and converted to a pickup. Often, as he goes about his business of hauling garbage, bears jump onto the back of Clarence's truck. He says it gives him great pleasure to sit inside and watch them scavenge for food amidst the garbage.

Clarence Larson and garbage truck

❧ CHAPTER 33 ❧

WHAT CAN'T YOU GET AT LOCKPORT?

The 1980s begin with George Jr. realizing that management of the resort, the sea villas and the ski area, is too much for him and he must cut back. After careful business analysis, he identifies the venture that has the most variables and the greatest risks versus potential rewards. Unfortunately, it is also the enterprise he loves most but in a gut-wrenching decision, he sells the ski area.

Within a few months, the new owner, Charles Skinner, announces multi-million dollar plans for the ski area. The plans include development of Moose Mountain to create the biggest vertical ski challenge in the Midwest. The building of condominiums also figures prominently. *"If condos are good elsewhere, why not in the beautiful ski hills of Lutsen?"* "Skinner asks. So begins what he calls *"...a whirlwind of hustling and bustling..."*

The following year, George Jr.'s cousin Willard decides to answer a question that has occurred to many people before and since: How did Lutsen get its name?

In pursuit of the answer, Willard travels to Europe. He knows the greatest King of Sweden, Gustavus II Adolphus, was killed during the Thirty Years War in a battle at Lutzen, Germany. Since Lutzen is at this time in East Germany and therefore behind the Iron Curtain, Willard seeks access to the town through a German lady who has special permission to travel there to visit relatives. Willard does not find much of interest in Lutzen but the lady gives him a souvenir map of the Lutzen battlefield.

Turning to Sweden, Willard and wife Dorothy travel to Norrkoping, hoping to find surviving relatives or records of his grandfather. En route to a relative's farm, they come upon a church, adorned with military ornaments. One of these is a cross of swords. There is a similar cross on the map Willard was given. He finds the church to be the burial site of local nobility with walls decorated with many coats of arms. He also finds documentation of Charles Nelson's baptism and learns of a nearby castle named Lofstad. Willard and Dorothy visit the castle and discover it was built by Count Axel Gustafson Lillie, a general in the army of King Gustavus II. The castle land was given to Lillie in honor of his service to the King.

During their stay, a local newspaper interviews the two visiting Americans and Willard mentions his disappointment at not finding his grandfather's farm. Local people then take him to the house where his grandfather was born. Originally situated on the Lofstad estate, the house, typical of a poor man's home in the 18th century, with squared-off timbers and a dirt floor, was sold to pay for upkeep of the castle. It was then removed log by log and rebuilt on the new owner's property.

Willard Nelson
on the steps of the house in Sweden where CAA was raised

Willard learns that Charles was born to a sharecropper on the castle estate when Count Carl Frederick Lillie resided there in 1863. Charles' first son, born in Minnesota, would be named Carl Frederick, indicating that perhaps Charles named his son after the Count.

Willard concludes that: *"My grandfather must have looked up to nobility in Sweden and so, when he came here, he made his castle, his Lofstad, which he thought he never could have. As time passed, Lutzen became Lutsen."* It honors, supposes Willard, the great king revered by Swedes, including Charles.

If Willard's supposition about his grandfather looking up to nobility is correct, it must have given CAA a twinge when he became a U.S. citizen and had to renounce and adjure forever all allegiance to the King.

Meanwhile, a death occurs in Washington State on October 3, 1981. The obituary sets the North Shore abuzz:

"Ida G Wethern age 93, oldest daughter of CAA and Anna Nelson, founders of Lutsen, passed away on Oct 3 at Everett WA where she had lived for the past 37 years. Ida was born in 1888 at Lutsen. She was the first white girl to be born in Cook County. (George Mayhew of Grand Marais was the first boy).

Ida served Lutsen as postmistress from approximately 1930 to 1942, when she moved to Everett. During WWI, she worked in Washington DC for Senator Borah and was selected by Cook County to christen the ship SS Cook, that was named as an honor to Cook County during the war, for having sold more war bonds per capita than any other county in the US. Lutsen led the drive to buy bonds in Cook County and the ship was originally to be named Lutsen but at the last moment was changed to SS Cook, to honor all of Cook County.

When Ida was a teenage girl, she took care of the little daughter of former Cook County Agriculture Agent William Clinch, whose wife had passed away. The girl's name was Christine – Christine Lake of the Honeymoon Trail is named after her. She moved east as a young girl and later married Jack Kelly. Their daughter Grace became an actress and is now known to the world as The Princess Grace of Monaco. Ida was invited to the wedding but was not able to attend."

A direct connection between the North Shore and Princess Grace seems unbelievable and on December 3, the News Herald confirms the inaccuracy:

"If you were one of those who were excited about this area's Princess Grace connection, well, the princess says it just ain't so.

*After the article appeared and after a little help from the library
to establish the proper form of address, we sent a copy of the
article to Her Serene Highness Princess Grace of Monaco. Last
Friday, we received the following communication through her
Chief Secretary, Choisit: "HSH Princess Grace has asked me to
thank you for your very kind letter of Nov 1, 1981, to which you
enclosed a clipping and to inform you that Christine Clinch is
not her mother. Mrs. John B. Kelly was born Margaret Majer."*

Lutsen earns several awards and plaudits in the early 1980s.
First, Nicholas Rowe, in a national publication, writes an article
entitled Ski Lodge Classics. In it, he chooses five favorite winter
vacation spots *"...where the skiing is as good as the atmosphere."*
The first resort he talks about is Lutsen: *"At the back door of
the lodge the woods are broken by only two roads, before
reaching the Arctic Circle. It is one of the remotest ski areas in
America and the only one in the world where surf breaks just
outside the bedroom window."*

Then, the Minnesota Society of the American Institute of
Architects presents several awards in recognition of architectural
excellence. A special 25-year award is presented to Lutsen
Resort. The award reads, *"Presented to Lutsen Resort for a
project of exceptional architectural merit, it demonstrates the
timeless characteristics of thoughtful and considered design.
Architect Edwin Lundie AIA, deceased, original owner George
Nelson Sr."*

Finally, in September 1983, a News Herald contributor
writes:

"Store Owners Give Unique Service

*What can't you get at Lockport? Well, as near as I can tell,
you can't get a free ride, tolerance for bad attitudes or an excuse
to wallow in self-pity. After all, this is Willie and Jo's livelihood
and the place where they spend most of their waking hours, so
there is no room for negative or destructive behavior. You are
expected to keep yourself and your children and whoever else is
with you, in line. You are treated with respect and dignity and
the same consideration is expected in return. I've been to the
store on only a few occasions but in a way, I have known
Lockport for a while. They represent to me all the positive*

things about people and life; honesty, caring, pride, dedication and plain old fashioned updated love for whatever you do and who you are. "

The Orwellian 1984 is a historic year for Lutsen. It is re-established as a township on July 2.

The resort is also being remade. The building housing the pool is completely renovated with a Swedish architectural theme, blending with the Lundie architecture of the lodge to create an aesthetically pleasing whole. Dehumidification equipment installed in the building allows the use of natural materials inside. The walls, ceiling and siding of the pool complex are cedar and the ceiling has massive wood beams. The pool is re-lined and river rock with the texture of small beach pebbles is used on the surrounding deck to complement the natural materials used in the building. A whirlpool is also installed.

Across the road from the resort, where the Lake Superior Touring Center was located the previous winter, is a new Lifesport Center. Open daily, the center is the hub of outdoor activities for the resort. Besides golf and tennis, several new services are offered, including bike rental, with all-terrain bikes suitable for unpaved surfaces. Canoes and accessories, day and weekend packs, rods and reels, and additional sporting goods, can also be rented or purchased. The Lifesport center is also the hub of operations for a summer naturalist at the resort who is developing a program of guided hikes and other structured activities and makes himself available as a natural history resource.

The resort also offers guests the possibility of acquiring an unusual memento. One such opportunity is afforded a guest who, one October day, observes a bull moose on the golf course. Nearby, a truck slows down to enter the resort grounds. The truck backfires and the moose bolts. In its flight, it trips over a cable, falls forward and breaks off its antlers. The DNR is called but no dead or injured moose is found. The guest is allowed to keep the antlers as a trophy.

143

❧ CHAPTER 34 ❧

THE GEM AT LUTSEN

In March of 1987, another major attraction is proposed for Lutsen. George Jr. is behind the plan for an 18-hole championship golf course to be built adjacent to the Lutsen Ski Hill. The 7,000 yard course will crisscross the Poplar River, playing up to the base of Moose Mountain and offering some of the most rugged and beautiful golfing scenery in the Midwest. If the necessary funding can be garnered, work will begin as early as the summer of 1988.

The project moves ahead quickly. Within a month, a bill related to course funding, is passed by a Minnesota House of Representatives committee. The bill creates a Joint Economic Development Authority with power to impose a 3% tax on hotel and resort accommodations in Lutsen, Tofte and Schroeder to help pay for the proposed golf course. The tax must be approved by area voters. Private financing will also be sought for the course and George Jr. will donate the land on which it will be built.

There are calls to build the course outside Lutsen, specifically in Tofte but no one is able or willing to provide the land, so that idea quickly fizzles.

During the summer, Cindy Nelson wins another sports trophy. She is surprised to do so because this trophy has nothing to do with skiing. It is a trophy for winning the Beaver Creek golf tournament. Cindy took up golf only one year earlier and previously entered a team tournament in Vail, Colorado, where she felt she played badly. Her motivation in entering the Beaver Creek tournament with the same partner, is to redeem herself. When she registers to play, the tournament director is at first unsure since all other entrants are men. *"Does that mean I cannot play?"* Cindy asks. After consulting the rulebook, the director says Cindy can participate but must use the men's tees. Even with that extra challenge, Cindy plays well. As the tournament winds down, the race is between Cindy's team and another team that includes Cindy's boss, the man who taught her golf. On hole 17, Cindy takes a huge swing at the ball and is mortified to see her drive go just 15 feet. The other team, however, does just as poorly and the teams end up in a playoff. At the awards ceremony Patti remarks that she thinks Cindy enjoyed winning this as much as her first ski trophy.

In early 1988, there are reports that Lutsen Resort is about to be sold. In response, George Jr. says, *"Lutsen Resort has not been sold, although it may be in the near future. The last two years have been very difficult and upsetting for our family. My wife Patti had heart surgery in June 1986 and then, in October of that year, we lost our son. I have cause to reflect on life, including my wife's and my retirement future. We would like to spend more time travelling and participating in the sports that we love, downhill and cross-country skiing, windsurfing, sailing, fishing and hunting. To do this, we need to get away from the day-to-day operations and the long-term financial responsibilities. We intend, however, to remain active in the community."*

George Jr. goes on to stress that the sale of the resort will not affect his donation of land for the golf course and states his intention to remain involved in seeing the project completed. *"The proposed new 18-hole golf course planned to be sited along the banks of the Poplar River is a top priority and I plan to be active until the golf course is a reality."*

The land that George Jr. will donate has been in his family for over 100 years and maintained in its virginal state along the lakeshore, Highway 61 and both banks of the Poplar River. Speaking for his family, George Jr. says, *"Our feeling for the land is twofold. First, we feel a stewardship to preserve and protect. Second, we are aware that the economic well-being of the North Shore does, to a considerable degree, depend on the use of the key land we control."* Not only will George Jr. donate the land, he will also pay the costs of transferring it to the county.

George Jr.'s giving does not stop at the golf course. Around the same time, he gives additional land to the Lutsen cemetery.

The ceremony at which George Jr. donates 328 acres of land for the golf course is held at the future site of the ninth hole, a rocky bluff overlooking the river. The site excites golf course architects because it lies along both banks of the Poplar River in a stretch that includes several falls and rapids. The golf course will have an inviting wild setting bordered to the North by the Lutsen Mountains Ski Area and to the South by Highway 61.

In the first week of March 1988, the Lutsen Resort, built and operated by the Nelson family for over a century, is sold. The new owner is the Lutsen Resort Company, formed by Scott Harrison and William Burns of Duluth. Their stated intention is to keep things as they are. To that end, George Jr. is retained as a consultant, with his daughter Becky and her husband Daryl Harris as managers. After the sale, George Sr. and Inga continue to live in an upstairs resort room.

Don Herfort, designer of several courses around the Midwest, is proposed as architect for the Lutsen project. Some of his most famous courses include Dellwood Hills, Indian Hills and River Oaks in suburban St. Paul: Como Park and Phalen Park in St. Paul: New Richmond Country Club, and Cumberland and Rhinelander in Wisconsin. His charge is to design a course that will be visually beautiful, challenging to championship caliber golfers but also enjoyable for everyday players. That fits with Herfort's own beliefs that *"Golf should be fun."* His large, flashed-sand bunkers and undulating greens are still a trademark of his work.

Bud Chapman, famous for his depictions of fictional, impossible golf holes, is named course artist.

However, hurdles remain. The project has yet to receive final approval from the state DNR. The town boards of Lutsen, Tofte and Schroeder still must approve several aspects of the project related to taxes and annual operating expenses. Construction bids need to be reviewed and contracts awarded. The Cook County Board must still issue bonds to fund construction.

All of these issues are eventually resolved and construction of the course begins with clearing the land. Crews encounter rocky areas but also a good supply of topsoil. This is a relief, since soil conditions are one of the project's great unknowns.

During construction, the course architect states that a bridge will be needed over the Poplar River but that it is not his responsibility to define exactly where the bridge should be. He does, however, define the area within which it must be located. An engineering firm in Minneapolis wants $15,000 to identify the bridge location, saying it will need to study river flow and water levels, including seasonal variations. The course budget is tight and that amount is not available. It is pointed out that the DNR has monitored the river for decades and information about flow and levels should be readily available. The company reduces its price to $10,000 but this is still too much. Mike Larson, one of the construction overseers, slips a can of spray paint into his pocket and takes George Jr. to the area identified by the course architect. He asks George Jr. where the bridge should be. Looking around, George Jr. studies some landmarks. He finally says, *"See that dark mark on that the big cedar tree over there? That is from the high water mark years ago. And over there is the pile of debris from the washout that occurred long ago. And here you can see where these trees were damaged by boulders coming down the river."* Based on these observations, George Jr. finally points to a spot on the riverbank and says, *"Build the bridge here."* Mike takes out his paint and sprays the spot.

In the 1998 "big blow down," seven inches of rain fall over several days. Mike wonders if the bridge has been swept away by the swollen Poplar River. He finds the river lapping at the underside of the bridge. Boulders are being swept down the river but pass below the bridge, which is undamaged. George Jr. had identified the perfect spot and at no cost.

When construction resumes in the spring, greens, tees and bunkers are quickly finished to lessen the threat of erosion. Regular applications of water and fertilizer allow the grass to quickly take hold. Other courses are playable in the fall after the spring they are planted but Lutsen has a short growing season and it is expected to be 18 months after planting before the course is playable. However, the grass grows so well that the course is playable the year after seeding. One thing the course lacks at this point is a name.

More critically, in October the project is still short some of its expected funding. It is decided to proceed anyway and the

Economic Development Authority closes on the land transfer with George Jr.

Another issue that has unexpectedly surfaced is resolved in early 1990. It is planned to take water from the Poplar River to keep the golf course grass green. However, the permit issued by the DNR sets minimum flow levels that do not allow taking water from a designated trout stream during late summer's typically low flows. The permit limitations make it impossible to water the course adequately in summer and course developers appeal the limitations. The Izaak Walton League becomes involved, questioning the statewide implications of allowing irrigation water to be drawn from a trout stream. As part of the political maneuvering, it is made known that legislation is being considered to remove the trout stream designation.

In a compromise solution, the DNR issues a revised permit, allowing the golf course to take water at a slower rate. The compromise allows the pumping of extra water during the summer of 1990 to facilitate initial seeding of the course. In subsequent years, if the river is low, only tees and greens can be watered. In 2011, however, a law is passed, allowing the ski area and resort to draw substantially more water from the Poplar River than it could take under the compromise. The issue of taking water from a designated trout stream, however, remains controversial and before the new law expires in 2016, the DNR and Lutsen are expected to study the river and make long-term decisions.

Meanwhile, funding issues continue. An expected grant from the State Department of Trade and Economic Development falls through. This leaves the project without funds to pay debts incurred for an entry road, septic and water utilities, underground electricity, and additional irrigation costs required by the DNR. Cook County is ultimately responsible for these debts and is faced with issuing additional bonds to cover the costs. State Representative Jim Oberstar is approached for help. He suggests that the U.S. Economic Development Authority would be the best place to get funding and points out *"For the North Shore, recreation is not just a nice thing to have to support the economy, it is the economy."* However, he also warns that the agency will not provide tourism funds. The agency does, however, support facilities. Since, without the funding, the clubhouse would be a modest structure and roads and parking would be unpaved, Cook County is really requesting facility support. The U.S. EDA field representative in Duluth agrees and submits the proposal for review and potential funding.

On August 13, 1990, an editorial in the News Herald summarizes what is at stake:

"$225,000 Problem – starting to worry.

First, there is the impact on the golf course project. Can there be a first class course with second grade facilities? Will golfers pay hefty greens fees for a dinky clubhouse with a gravel parking lot? Second, where will the money come from? Will county taxpayers have to dig deep?"

The newspaper further notes that there is still no name for the course and administration specifics such as greens fees, dues and clubhouse management have not been worked out, although the course is expected to open in the summer of 1991.

Within two months, that opening date is in jeopardy. There has been a washout from heavy rain and 4,500 ft of underground piping has failed and needs to be replaced. While not optimistic about 1991, the developers think the course could open towards the end of that summer if there is good grass-growing weather. However, 1992 seems a more likely opening date. On a brighter note, they have received good reports from golfers who have looked over the course. Based on these reports, there is optimism that revenues might exceed projections.

The wild side of the golf course is already exceeding expectations. In May, 1991, a cinnamon sow-bear with two cubs, one black, the other cinnamon, shows up and lays claim to territory around the third green. The same bears had been fed by construction workers the previous summer. One day they discover a lunch bucket and devour the contents. There is a small pond near the third green and the bears like to play there every day. Their den is uncovered three to four feet from the seventh tee, under a birch stump. The sow has spent the winter and borne the cubs there.

The adult bear reappears the following year, this time with triplets, one black and two cinnamons. The bears' new den is in the roots of an old spruce tree between the driving range and hole 18. The Herald edition of May 11, 1992, reports the impacts the bears are having:

"Wonder what the P.G.A. rules manual says about cub bear hazards on a golf course?

Maybe the association will have to come up with a special amendment to cover the situation this spring at the Superior National Golf Course at Lutsen.

The first weekend the course was open, two young fellows from St. Paul came back to the clubhouse and told Greg Leland, the golf pro, about bear problems on fairway No. 11.

They said that after they teed off on No. 11, the cub bears came out of the woods, picked up their golf balls and began playing with them.

The cubs were accompanied by the cinnamon sow bear who has been hanging around Superior National for three years now, this spring bringing forth three cubs – two cinnamon and one black.

The city slickers from St. Paul, instead of dropping new balls for a no-penalty bear hazard, high-tailed it back to the clubhouse and demanded a refund.

Leland said they didn't want to take a rain check. Since they had already played the front nine, he returned half of their greens fee. The pro said that some time later, a couple playing behind the two from St. Paul, recovered two golf balls, somewhat the worse for wear and all chewed up by the cubs. Kevin Twiest, who works at the course, says he found more evidence of bear activity the other day.

He says he was mowing the grass and found the marker for the No. 14 tee near the green on No. 13.

The marker, made of wood, is round and painted white. It is about three inches in diameter.

Twiest said there were small teeth marks on it, evidence that one of the cubs had picked it up and carried it toward the green on No. 13."

*Mother bear and three cubs
out for a stroll around the
Superior National Golf Course in Lutsen*

On June 3, 1991, the golf course is finally christened. A naming contest produces a winner when *Superior National at Lutsen* is chosen as the name. Among other names seriously considered were: The Lynx at Lutsen, The Poplar River Golf Course and The Lutsen Mountain Golf Course.

Surprisingly, it is announced that the course will open August 15, with play initially limited to nine holes and a mobile trailer serving as a temporary clubhouse. Even though financing is still an issue, it is felt that construction of a permanent clubhouse must begin before the fall frost.

Accordingly, the County is asked to issue bonds. The amount needed has swollen to $405,000. It is pointed out that without a proper clubhouse, the entire undertaking is at risk and, if everything collapses, it will fall on Cook County taxpayers. The county commissioners, faced with unattractive options, ask for more time to consider the request.

The News Herald is scathing in its assessment of the situation. A September 16 editorial castigates the developers for "*counting chickens*" and not giving any thought to contingencies for construction. Hence, *"...just enough chicks had hatched to build a beautiful golf course without a clubhouse"* and *"...the project demonstrated the need to think carefully before government got involved in projects that should be private."* At the same time, the newspaper acknowledges that the course needs a first rate clubhouse and amenities. *"Doing business out of a mobile trailer will not cut it and there is no way to finance a clubhouse without a second bond issue."* The newspaper concludes that, with $2.1 million already at risk, the County has virtually no choice. *"After all, what is another $405,000?"*

Within a week, a General Obligation Bond issue is approved. In reality, the 3% sales tax pays off the bonds and the county never has to put up any money. Clubhouse construction begins in the fall.

Some comfort is taken from the fact that the golf course is drawing large crowds and revenues are ahead of projections. In its first two months, the course takes in more than 30% of the revenue expected in its first full year of operations. This is impressive since there has been no major promotion of the course. So successful would the golf course be, that over time, 30% of Cook County's tax revenue would come from there. That success would continue despite competitors such as Giant's Ridge, which is state funded and Thunder Bay, Canada, which has access to gambling revenue.

An interesting finding is that a surprising number of Canadians visit the Lutsen course. Over 40% of golfers are from north of the border. This presents an issue related to handling next year's customers; the course is obliged to give priority to Cook County residents but many Canadians travel a long way to spend money at Lutsen.

In June 1992, a study estimates the economic impact of the golf course. Construction has contributed $2.3 million to the local economy and yielded 34 jobs. Visitor expenditures during one full golf season will contribute $5.6 million in new direct expenditures and create 200 permanent jobs within Cook

County. The study also notes that the golf course will likely lead to the construction of 350 vacation homes, generating $16.7 million in income and creating 564 jobs during construction. There will also be significant income to taxing authorities through property, lodging, fuel, income, corporate income, and sales taxes.

This may have impressed the federal EDA. In early November, the agency approves the plans and specifications for a clubhouse, irrigation system and parking lot and issues a $265,200 grant.

On Sunday, March 21, 1993, George Nelson, Sr. dies at the Cook County Nursing Home in Grand Marais at age 93. His obituary notes that George worked at various times as a commercial fisherman, game warden with dog sled and school bus driver. It also says, in part:

"Mr. Nelson was a true North Shore pioneer. His determination and skill carried the Lodge through two major fires. His legacy is the world famous resort enjoyed by thousands each year. He was active in many organizations including the Minnesota Resort Owners Association, the Cook County Chamber of Commerce and the local Masonic Lodge. He was a founding member of the Lutsen Evangelical Lutheran Church."

In the spring of 1994 the Lutsen Scientific and Natural Area is created. Located near Eagle Mountain and set aside for recreation and scientific research, the area contains many old-growth trees, including: maples over 200 years old, white birch over 150 years old, black ash over 165 years old, and 15 acres of virgin white cedar, some over 300 years old.

The success of the Superior National Golf Course can be seen from the following items printed in the Herald:

Editorial excerpt from the edition of October 3, 1994:

"Superior National is a major asset

No one can deny that Superior National has been a financial success or that it is becoming a favorite destination for golfers from all over the map: It is doubtful that anyone who lives in Cook County has not heard rave reviews from visitors to the shore who play the links. If one travels out of the county, it is rare not to hear someone comment about how beautiful and well run the golf course is. Of course, the positive ripple effect for businesses, while hard to measure precisely, is tremendous. Hotels and restaurants gift shops and gas stations - everyone has spin-off business due to Superior National. Even the Gunflint Hills course, an excellent facility its own right, has benefited from greater golfing. Our hats are off to the county board, EDA, RMC and all those involved with the development and outstanding operation of the Superior National Golf Course. Congratulations."

The Herald edition of October 10, 1994 reports the dedication of the course:

"Honor George Nelson — Superior National Dedication

Most people hope that someday, when their lives are finished, they can leave a legacy for others. Maybe something that makes the world a little better off than before.

So on Wednesday, October 12, the official dedication of the Superior National Golf Course at Lutsen will be made in memory of George Nelson Sr. and George (Nibs) Nelson III. The Nelson family donated the land to Cook County for the purpose of building the golf course. One only has to visit the course to see that the Nelsons' generosity has been rewarded with a fine facility.

The fairways and greens sit in one of the most beautiful settings imaginable, with views of Lake Superior from countless vantage points, fantastic hills and valleys, and Moose Mountain and Eagle Mountain in the background.

The fairway on the ninth hole provides a perfect perch to see the course in all its splendor. The left side of it rises to a point well above the fairway. It is almost a cliff, but not quite, since it is landscaped and mowed all the way to the top. Standing there, one sees a vista that is breathtaking. Off in the distance lie Superior and the hilltops that guard her. One sees stands of pine and spruce and birch and maple in every fold of a landscape that tilts toward the valley just below. And there, the Poplar River flows endlessly among the rocks. A red fox moves by, made cautious by people's presence.

You see moose there sometimes, and bears too. It is idyllic. Perhaps as fine a legacy as one could ever wish for.

So Wednesday, there will be a dedication."

One October 17, 1994, letter to the editor states:

"The Gem at Lutsen

On a recent trip to the North Shore, I found a gem. It is large and green with many interesting contours. In places, it reflected the sun but when I inspected it more closely, it had a variety of colors. I am not talking of some rare stone pushed to the surface. In fact, this was not a mineral at all but a man-made oasis called Superior National Golf Course. I have played many courses in Minnesota and I have not seen a course more beautifully designed and maintained. Cook County, you have something in Superior National Golf Course that will serve you for generations to come. Superior National is a true gem in the north woods.

Sincerely,

A.W. Brown, owner, Birch View Golf Course, Nisswa, Minnesota."

Superior National Golf Course

The year ends on a sad note when Inga dies on December 16.

Since the days when CAA arrived in Minnesota, the North Shore has seen many significant changes. Among those that posed serious challenges to people living in the region were the demise of the commercial fishing industry, the loss of lake traffic and transportation, and the disappearance of small farms that used to be an economic factor in the area.

However, other trends provided opportunities, including the creation and ongoing improvement of roads, the rise of tourism as a major industry, the advent and widespread use of telephones and better fire and health protection. The Nelsons were often the instigators of progress but always utilized it to improve Lutsen and the North Shore.

In return, they were and continue to be stewards of the land. They have maintained a development-free area of land stretching three miles north of Highway 61 and along two miles of Lake Superior shoreline. The only other areas on the North Shore protected from development are 88 acres in the Encampment Forest under the protection of the Minnesota Land Trust, and in the Grand Portage Reservation.

In short, CAA's descendents still remember that Lutsen has been good to them and they intend to continue being good to Lutsen.

☙ CHAPTER 35 ☙

MEMORIES

Following are recollections of past events in and around Lutsen. First, CAA's grandson Willard Nelson recalls growing up in Lutsen. Then, Glenn Devery, an outdoors writer, tells of an experience he had with Willard's father, Carl, on Caribou Lake. Finally, a young Minneapolis resident describes what it was like to work at the resort in the early 1970s.

Memories of Willard Charles Nelson

Some of my earliest memories are of being alone while my siblings attended school. I must have been a handful for my mom because eventually she asked if I could sit in the classroom, even though I was much younger than the pupils. I remember the school had one room for grades one through eight. There were no women teachers back then. I think sitting in class early made me more advanced than the other kids when I actually began school.

We kids also had chores to do. One of these involved helping with the building of a huge fireplace in our living room. My mother selected individual rocks from the Lake Superior shore below our house. My brother Harold and I had to carry the rocks in gunnysacks up the hill to our house. I believe the selected rocks can only be found at that spot and at one other beach east of Grand Marais. Harold and I suffered many bruises, scrapes and blisters from hauling all those rocks.

Of course, medical care was very different back then. In the very early days, there were no doctors and people treated themselves, or they lived with whatever ailed them, or they died. Dr. Hicks was the first doctor we had. He lived in Grand Marais. Later, I remember a Dr. Smith who made house calls. There was no medical insurance; you were expected to pay cash.

One major medical emergency we had involved a shooting:

My father used to store his hunting rifle on a set of deer antlers that was mounted high on the wall of our living room.

157

Regrettably, he never locked the trigger because we kids could not reach that high.

One day, a teenage girl from the resort came to visit mother, who was somewhere outside at that moment. The girl came inside to wait. She was tall enough to reach the gun and took it down to show my two and a half year-old sister, Dorothea. The gun went off and the child was shot, the bullet entering behind an ear and exiting through her forehead.

The sound brought my mother running into the house. Seeing her daughter shot on the floor, the distraught woman believed her dead and ran off to drown herself in Lake Superior. My dad, who had also been outside, had to drag her off the beach and take her to the resort where my grandma looked after her.

The doctor was summoned from Grand Marais but he pronounced my sister dead. Her body was laid out in the Swedish tradition and since the deceased was not allowed to be alone, my dad sat up with the body. In the kerosene lamplight, he saw the shroud move and removed it. My sister looked up at him and asked for her teddy bear. No bandages had been applied until my dad applied some then.

My sister was taken by boat to Grand Marais where the doctor's wife looked after her for three weeks. She made a full recovery and went on to have several children of her own. The teenage girl vanished amid all the commotion and was never seen again.

FINS & FEATHERS MAGAZINE - AUGUST 1976

Ol' Carl and the Tourist Bear
By Glenn Devery

I had the world by the tail that summer as a fishing guide on a pristine lake nestled in the pine and spruce wilderness of northern Minnesota. And then one day I got more than I'd bargained for....

Long before I discovered Portage Resort, Carl Nelson had built his place on the neck of a peninsula that balloons into Caribou Lake, five hilly miles inland from Lutsen on Lake Superior. The rustic log cabins had an icebox -- not a refrigerator -- and every winter Ol' Carl hand-cut a supply of ice blocks from the lake to be preserved in sawdust for the next season.

I went down to the icehouse late one afternoon and had just locked the steel tongs into a block of ice.

As I lifted it out of the wet sawdust and reached for the hose to wash it off - BANG! A rifle shot exploded the summer stillness.

The surprise blast nearly made me drop the ice. But before the last echo faded across the lake, I had jumped around the corner to see a black bear limping into the timber.

The new man in Cabin Five spotted me and whooped: "A bear! Big one! Right outside my cabin!"

Ol' Carl popped out of the resort store across the road and roared: "Dammit all! It's fishin' season, not huntin' season!" and his gravelly voice fairly shook the surrounding pines.

He marched briskly over to the cabin where the excited "bear hunter" stood in the open door, still clutching his rifle in both hands. For a few seconds, Carl stared at him in silent disbelief. His gaze bounced from the animated tourist to the bullet hole in the window. Then, watching the end of the rifle barrel, he took a cautious step to one side and asked incredulously: "Right through the glass?"

"C-C-Criminy! I wasn't t-taking any chances with a b-b-bear," stammered the tourist. "Course I'll pay for the window."

Carl had no comment on that, and plainly it was the least of his worries. "He was jest after the bacon smell," he apologized for the bear. "Would've run off when you slammed the screen door."

The young man began to look a little sheepish, and Ol' Carl told him not to fret about it, but to please put that dangerous weapon away. "You sure you hit him?" Carl was anxious to know.

"I think so," the tourist replied meekly. "He fell down, but got right up again, and...."

People gathered around to see what all the fuss was about, and the trigger-happy tourist elaborated on his role of public defender.

I followed Ol' Carl over to the store in silence. When we were inside he went directly behind the counter and reached underneath to a secret niche for a pint of spirits that he kept hidden from his wife, Pheobe. And this time he tilted his head back for a quick gulp of nerve medicine without even looking out the window first to see if she was around. He ran the top of his hand across his mouth and didn't say anything, and I was afraid I knew what he had in mind.

"I'm just afraid I know which bear that was," Carl said quietly. "Afraid I do."

"They don't bother nobody if ya leave 'em alone," he mused half to himself. "Bear wounded's a different story. Be kind o' dangerous for somebody to stumble onto him if we don't ketch him first."

I had no comment on his understatement-of-the-year, and wasn't sure I liked the way he said "we." Following a wounded bear trail in the green of summer didn't make my list of regular duties.

Ol' Carl continued: "Years ago, a lumberjack friend o' mine purt' near stepped on a bear that was poor-shot by some hunter. It was restin' under a windfall. Fella didn't have any gun, jest an axe. That bear lit into him, but he was handy with a blade 'n it saved his life. He was plain lucky to git away, clawed up some and with a broken arm."

That did nothing toward stirring the hero blood in me.

Thoughtfully, Ol' Carl took a fresh pinch of snuff and peered out the window at the setting sun. Putting it off until tomorrow would be too risky. He pushed back his wilted all-weather hat to scratch his head, and his scraggly grey hair bristled like a clump of frosted pine needles. Then he reached for a flashlight and his battered rifle, a .22 caliber model that belonged in an antique collection. As we left the resort store, Pheobe called to him from their cabin on the lakeshore. Carl squinted in her direction, but didn't hear what she said. He just waved, and we were off.

Neither of us said anything for a while, and I thought back to the young gun-toting tourist's arrival three days before...

When we were showing the young couple their quarters in Cabin 5 that morning, Ol' Carl had chuckled as he pointed down the path to the outhouse behind the cabin: "Never lost a customer to a bear yet!" and he nudged me in the ribs.

The tourists did not look assured.

Pheobe managed a wan smile at her husband's favorite joke and went about showing the newly arrived couple where to find everything.

Carl could never get around to converting the cabins to inside plumbing - it would have taken away his pet "tourist" gag.

All the same, that time his woodsy humor was wasted on the two young vacationers. "You mean there's a bear around here?" asked the man soberly, and his wife stood by in wide-eyed silence. "Several of 'em," Ol' Carl replied with little concern. "Bears are sort o' like most neighbors - leave 'em be and they won't bother you."

The black bears were sometimes a nuisance at night, raiding garbage cans around the cabins, and yet he saw no reason to alarm the new guests. Ordinarily, he would have mentioned the dump area a mile down the road, a favored spot for night "bear watching." Visitors could gather there in the safety of their cars to observe the scavenging bruins in the headlights.

The new couple forgot about bears that first day and went fishing. They didn't catch anything, but the next boat in had over the legal limit. Ol' Carl admired their excessive catch for a minute, then hinted: "Wouldn't want the game warden to spoil your vacation...." And the surplus walleyes, which he neatly filleted, found their way to the less fortunate Cabin Five tourists' frying pan. (Carl always referred to people as tourists -- though not unkindly - unless they were permanent residents of the North Country).

He smelled of woodsmoke and pine pitch, and most everybody called him "Ol' Carl," in a way that showed hidden affection. On the surface, he was as rough as the bark of a Norway pine, but after you got under his coarse veneer, you'd never find a truer friend. He was like an extra grandfather to me, and now I was committed to follow the old-timer into the darkening woods in search of a wounded bear.

He knew the terrain: after all, as a young boy he had served as a hunting guide in these parts.

We climbed a hill through scattered birches standing like slim ghosts aglow in the twilight. And when we paused to catch our breath, the eerie cry of a loon drifted up from the lake below. After going through a bog and a stand of tamaracks, we entered heavier undergrowth, and slowed down to pick our way between tangles of alder and dogwood brush. Occasionally we found tell-tale red spots on the leaves. In spite of my great respect for Ol' Carl's command of woodlore, I knew he needed bifocals to read a newspaper - although he would never admit to any such infirmity. Without a doubt, the bear's senses would be more keen than all ours combined.

If Ol' Carl felt any animosity toward the tourist who caused this dilemma, he didn't show it. I followed him into the thick underbrush and wondered why he didn't take a bigger weapon, and why *I* hadn't thought of bringing along a gun, or a knife - *anything*.

He seemed to know by instinct where the bear was headed, even before we picked up the scant blood trail. I guessed aloud at how badly the bear might be wounded, but the native woodsman grunted his unconcern. "Looks like he's headed for the swamp," he sang out with no attempt at keeping his voice down. And he eagerly took the lead with that ancient single-shot rifle.

Under the circumstances, I was sure it got dark a whole lot faster that night, and we had to move very carefully to follow the trail. By the time Ol' Carl switched on his flashlight, I was ready to turn tail and race back to the resort! It was one of those thick lens types and he had to thump it a few times before the light came on, the weak batteries producing a glimmer equal to one lighted candle at best. From then on we had to be constantly alert to any strange sounds of the woods.

The short-sleeved shirt I wore offered no protection against the hostile brush that raked my bare arms. And the scratches only heightened my mental picture of how it could feel to be clawed by a mad bear.

The dense forest suggested to me that we whisper anything necessary to the search. Contrarily, you'd have thought we were merely hunting rabbits in the daytime, the way Ol' Carl boomed out: "Pears like he's slowin' down some..."

We crept along tediously, and during a lull in our one-sided conversation, suddenly a twig snapped. Carl put his hand on my arm – as if I needed any warning to stand still! I already had a death grip on the nearest sapling. Silent seconds went by, then under his breath he said, "Only a deer."

We moved on, and a few minutes later - when my nerves were almost back to normal - there was a flurry of crackling brush ahead of me. Carl dropped the flashlight and the world went black. He let out a holler and I turned to cold stone. In a second or two that seemed like an hour, he rasped, "Porcupine! Almost stepped on him." At this point, I volunteered that maybe we should go back and get a better flashlight, and more men, and some dogs, and....

"Naw...can't be much further. Looka' that splotch there," he claimed, holding the feeble light close to the ground. "We'll find him purty soon."

"More likely he'll find us pretty soon," I mumbled limply.

Ol' Carl either didn't hear me or he chose to ignore my pessimism, and we inched our way deeper into the black woods.

A short time later, Carl stopped in front of a big fallen tree trunk and kept quiet. Cautiously, he peeked over the top into the broken branches, with the dying flashlight in one hand and his gun in the other. By now it was so dark I couldn't have seen a luminous polar bear. I had an urge to offer to hold the light.

With outstretched hand and open mouth, I just stood there. This is it, I thought. What a fine place for a wounded bear to hide and wait for his pursuers. I froze, waiting for the angry bear to charge.

The ominous hush ended abruptly with the crack of Carl's rifle, and all was quiet again. By the time he spoke, my feet were back on the ground, and I remembered to breathe.

"Thought I'd better make sure the pore critter was out of his misery," he stated simply.

"Kind o' what I figgered..." his voice trailed off as he sat down on the log to rest. " It was 'Stumpy'... lost his left front paw in a trap some time ago. Guess I must've chased him away from the garbage cans a hunnert times..."

We both just sat there a while. I couldn't see his face, but there was something in his voice that told me a lot about how Carl felt about what he had just had to do.

When we got back to the resort, a worried Pheobe was still up. Her snow-white hair glowed in the light of the cabin door as she stepped out to count heads. While Carl tried to assure her that he was still in one piece, I bid them good night and headed for my bunk.

Next morning, the couple in Cabin Five decided to get back to civilization, and the young man came over to the store to pay his bill. Ol' Carl, as cheerful as ever, showed no hard feelings about the previous night's bear hunt. The tourist had very little to say - and nothing at all to say about bears. As their car went over the hill out of sight, Carl said quietly: "Kind o' feel sorry for him... Fella like that is way out o' place up here."

The dust had hardly settled when another car came into camp. Carl and Pheobe greeted the new people warmly and showed them to Cabin Five. Ol' Carl winked in my direction as he pointed to the little house out back: "Never lost a customer to a bear yet!" he grinned.

Author note – The Portage Resort was so-named because a band of Chippewa used to have a summer campground and portage on the site.

<u>Memories of Judy Peterson</u>

I was excited about my new job as a waitress at Lutsen Resort - my first job away from home. I took off in my parents' 1969 Buick LaSabre. The drive was about three hours. On arrival, I was shown my quarters on the first floor of a bunkhouse at the top of the hill. All staff lived there. Some guests stayed on the floor above.

A hostess gave new staff classes in how to serve people. We had to vacuum and clean the chairs. When not working, we were on our own to sleep, explore or wash our uniforms in the resort laundry.

The kitchen always had a few leftovers for staff. The baker made fresh bread, pies, and other desserts daily.

I enjoyed meeting the people I served. People I waited on always wanted to know about the fish. Someone went out daily and got the catch. Bluefin was one of the specialties. I'll never forget the first time I took trout to someone and they were surprised to get the head served to them.

There were many people from other countries. Some I could barely understand. I enjoyed listening to Canadian accents. The excitement of the surroundings and the people lured me back to work in the winter.

The Nelsons were long time skiers. Their daughter, Cindy was an Olympic medalist and her parent and grandparents went skiing almost every day. They came in for breakfast and then hit the slopes. I was hoping to learn how to ski during my three weeks working there.

My only problem was I didn't have skis. One of the girls had a set of skis, boots and poles she said I could use. I was nervous trying to get the bindings around the boots. They weren't the fancy kind we now have. Once I got the skis on, my next attempt was to get up the hill. To get up the bunny hill meant using the rope tow. Unfortunately, I didn't have leather gloves, which made the rope slip through my hands. I got about half way up and then let go and struggled to get away from the tow to a space where I wouldn't be in anyone's way. There were two of us in about the same shape: no experience and very low-tech equipment. We wobbled down the hill using our snowplow *technique. It was not a pretty sight. Every time we fell, we left a blue imprint in the snow from our denim jeans.*

My next time out, I rented skis and got better gloves. This made a huge difference. I graduated to some hills with chair lifts and thought I was really making progress. Then I tried Greasy Gulch. It was an area with a catwalk to another chair. On my way across the gulch, I split my pants. Since I had long underwear and a long coat, I decided to tough it out and skied for another couple of hours.

Some waiters and waitresses had places close to Lutsen and hosted parties, which we all enjoyed. Some played guitar at the bar in Lutsen and played for us at the parties. I'd never been with a more eclectic group of people. They were from California, Michigan, Minneapolis, and small towns across the North Country.

After Christmas, things slowed down and I took the bus back to Minneapolis.

🐾 CHAPTER 36 🐾

FAMOUS PEOPLE

The following celebrities stayed at the Lutsen Resort:

Nelson Rockefeller - skied with friends from Minneapolis.

Doctors Charles and Will Mayo - frequent visitors.

Agnes Moorhead - actress, stopped overnight on her way to Port Arthur (and paid with a check that bounced).

Arthur Godfrey and family.

Lowell Thomas

Doctor Billy Graham

Sinclair Lewis

It is also rumored that **John Dillinger** and **Al Capone** hid out at the resort. Capone is said to have stayed in a cabin where he shot some holes in a wall. CAA supposedly demanded and received compensation for the damage.

PHOTOGRAPHS - CREDITS

The following photographs are published with permission from the Cook County Historical Society:

Page 9 - Nelson family
Page 24 - Mail sleigh
Page 47 - Dock at Lockport
Page 70 - Dining room
Page 76 – Fountain

The following photographs were previously published in the Cook County News Herald (with dates, when known):

Page 2 - CAA and dog
Page 12 - Fishermen in icy boat
Page 13 - Ankle deep in herring
Page 16 – Lake Superior ice field
Page 114 – Lutsen Volunteer Fire Dept (pub 12/23/1976)
Page 116 - Drawing of church (pub 5/16/1957)
Page 124 - Drawing of new chalet (pub 12/02/1965)
Page 133 - Alpine slide (pub 08/18/1977)
Page 136 - Simba the lion (pub 03/09/1978)
Page 137 - Skiing Sheik (pub 03/30/1978)
Page 140 - Willard Nelson in Sweden (pub 07/23/1981)
Page 151 - Bear and three cubs (pub 05/18/1992)

Other photographs were provided by George Nelson Jr.

Robert Mc Dowell

HISTORY - CREDITS

Some of the history reported in the book is based on articles written by Willard Nelson and published in the **Cook County News Herald** as noted below:

Book reference---is based on an article titled---published on
Page 25---THE DANGERS OF DELIVERING MAIL---07/06/1992
Page 37---THE STORY OF AN OLD CAMP FOUND---09/14/1992
Page 42---THE BIG MOOSE CANNING BEE---10/12/1992
Page 46---THE GREAT LUTSEN RAILROAD---08/24/1992
Page 67---THE ONE-MOOSE POWERED SKIFF---02/14/2003

Made in the USA
Columbia, SC
09 June 2022

61492499R00100